God's Daily Promises

DAILY WISDOM
FROM GOD'S WORD

BOOKS IN THE
GOD'S DAILY PROMISES SERIES

God's Daily

PROMISES

DAILY WISDOM
FROM GOD'S WORD

Tyndale House Publishers, Inc.

Carol Stream, Illinois

Visit Tyndale's exciting Web site at www.tyndale.com

TYNDALE and Tyndale's quill logo are registered trademarks of Tyndale House Publishers, Inc.

God's Daily Promises: Daily Wisdom from God's Word

General Editors: Ron Beers and Amy Mason

Contributing Editor: Rebecca Beers

Contributing Writers: V. Gilbert Beers, Ronald A. Beers, Brian R. Coffey, Jonathan Farrar, Jonathan Gray, Shawn A. Harrison, Sandy Hull, Rhonda K. O'Brien, and Douglas J. Rumford

Designed by Julie Chen

Edited by Michal Needham

ISBN-13: 978-1-4143-1230-9
ISBN-10: 1-4143-1230-X

Printed in the United States of America

13 12 11 10 09 08 07
 7   6   5   4   3   2   1

INTRODUCTION

Why did God make so many promises? Maybe it's
because he wants to show you how much you can
really trust him. Maybe he is so interested in you that
he is trying to get your attention with each amazing promise he makes, wanting to show you just
how much you have to look forward to as you travel
through life. This unique book presents more
than 365 of these incredible promises, at least one
for every day of the year. All these promises will
come true—or have already come true. You simply have to decide whether you want to be part of
them or not.

Imagine that every morning you could be
inspired by a promise from God's Word and
then live the rest of the day with either the expectation that God will fulfill that promise or the
confidence that comes from a promise already
fulfilled. *God's Daily Promises* is designed to
inspire you in just that way. Every page is
dated, making the book easy to use. First,
read the promise from God. Think about it.
Let it soak in. Then read the short devotional
note to help you look at your day differently
because of God's promise. Finally, read
the question at the end to encourage and
motivate you to trust that this promise was
meant for you. Claim the promise as your
own with the confidence that you can always

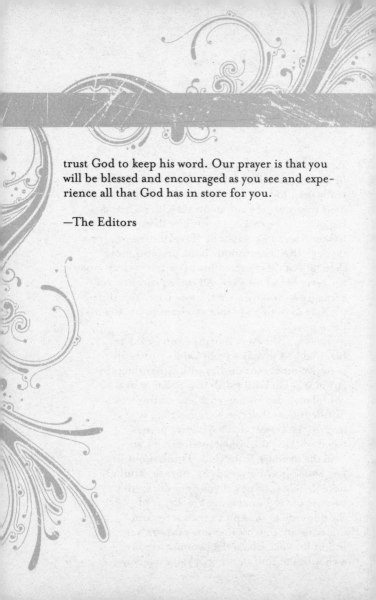

trust God to keep his word. Our prayer is that you will be blessed and encouraged as you see and experience all that God has in store for you.

—The Editors

JANUARY

JANUARY 1

BEGINNINGS

TODAY'S PROMISE

Great is his faithfulness; his mercies begin afresh each morning.

—LAMENTATIONS 3:23

TODAY'S THOUGHT

Life is a series of beginnings, and how you enter into them makes all the difference. Although the thought of new beginnings sometimes makes you feel anxious, remember that you experience them all the time. Each day brings a whole series of new opportunities, including opportunities to get to know God better and to start over with a new attitude toward circumstances and people in your life. God's mercy toward you is new every day, no matter what you've done or how you've treated him or other people the day before. That means you don't have to be burdened by yesterday's failures or regrets.

TODAY'S PLAN

Do you give new mercies each day to the people you live and work with, just as God gives new mercies to you?

BEGINNINGS

TODAY'S PROMISE

Create in me a clean heart, O God. Renew a loyal spirit within me.   —PSALM 51:10

TODAY'S THOUGHT

You harvest what you plant. Pumpkin seeds produce pumpkins. Sunflower seeds produce sunflowers. If you have sinful desires and thoughts, it is evidence that some bad seeds have been planted in your heart, and you need to do some weeding. You must beg the Lord to plant within you a clean heart so that your life will produce clean thoughts, motives, and actions. Complete renewal cannot be accomplished yet. None of us will be entirely "clean" in this life, but one of the most worthy goals you can pursue this year is purity of mind and heart.

TODAY'S PLAN

Can you make purity of mind and heart your goal for today? What might you look like a year from now—inside and out—if you met this goal not just today but every day?

CALL OF GOD

TODAY'S PROMISE

I knew you before I formed you in your mother's womb. Before you were born I set you apart and appointed you as my prophet to the nations.

—JEREMIAH 1:5

TODAY'S THOUGHT

You might think that God was only speaking to the prophet Jeremiah in these verses. But God calls everyone to do a certain job, to accomplish a specific task, or to use his or her gifts in a unique way. When God calls you to do something, he will make sure you know what it is. Often you will feel a strong sense of leading from him. It's up to you to respond and walk through the door of opportunity he opens.

TODAY'S PLAN

Do you have a strong sense that God is leading you in a certain direction or asking you to serve him in some way? How can you begin to respond to God's call in practical ways today?

GIFTS

TODAY'S PROMISE

There are different kinds of spiritual gifts, but the same Spirit is the source of them all. There are different kinds of service, but we serve the same Lord. God works in different ways, but it is the same God who does the work in all of us. —1 CORINTHIANS 12:4-6

TODAY'S THOUGHT

The natural abilities you have are gifts from God, and they are often a clue to what God wants you to do. Would God give you certain talents and spiritual gifts and then not ask you to use them? You may have natural gifts in the area of cooking, entertaining, managing a business, teaching, handling money, playing an instrument, or any number of other things. Use whatever gifts you have to bring honor and glory to God. Then you will be right where you need to be to discover God's will for you and to accomplish his purpose for you.

TODAY'S PLAN

How is God calling you to serve him with your gifts in the coming year?

PRAYER

TODAY'S PROMISE

Keep on asking, and you will receive what you ask for. Keep on seeking, and you will find. Keep on knocking, and the door will be opened to you. For everyone who asks, receives. Everyone who seeks, finds. And to everyone who knocks, the door will be opened.

—MATTHEW 7:7-8

TODAY'S THOUGHT

There's more to prayer than just getting an answer to a question or a solution for a problem. God often does more in your heart through your act of prayer than he does in the actual answer to your prayer. As you persist in talking and listening to God, he promises that you will gain greater understanding of yourself and your situation as well as God's purpose for you and his direction for your life.

TODAY'S PLAN

How can you make your prayer life more of a conversation with God?

FUTURE

TODAY'S PROMISE

"I know the plans I have for you," says the Lord. "They are plans for good and not for disaster, to give you a future and a hope." —JEREMIAH 29:11

TODAY'S THOUGHT

Many people picture God as stern and vindictive, just watching and waiting for the chance to zap humans with bolts of misfortune. But this verse shows the opposite. God loves you and wants only good things for you. He wants your future—both in this life and in heaven—to be bright and hopeful.

TODAY'S PLAN

How can you begin to recognize God's goodness all around you?

BIBLE

TODAY'S PROMISE

All Scripture is inspired by God and is useful to teach us what is true and to make us realize what is wrong in our lives. It corrects us when we are wrong and teaches us to do what is right. God uses it to prepare and equip his people to do every good work.

—2 TIMOTHY 3:16-17

TODAY'S THOUGHT

If you buy a new computer but neglect to read the instruction manual, you'll miss out on many of the functions the machine is capable of doing. You'll be operating with just enough knowledge to perform basic functions. When it comes to reading the Bible, most of us read just enough to get by. We miss so much of what God's Word has to offer. Read the Bible daily so you can thoroughly understand everything God wants you to know. Then you will be able to live at peak performance.

TODAY'S PLAN

What can you do to develop the habit of reading God's Word more regularly?

PATIENCE

TODAY'S PROMISE

The Holy Spirit produces this kind of fruit in our lives: . . . patience. —GALATIANS 5:22

TODAY'S THOUGHT

If you've ever spent two hours stuck in rush-hour traffic or held a crying baby at two o'clock in the morning, you know something about patience. According to the Bible, patience is a form of perseverance and endurance that allows you to respond to frustrating circumstances with grace and self-control. Contrary to popular opinion, patience is not merely a personality trait; it is a by-product of the presence and work of the Holy Spirit in the heart and mind of the believer. God promises that when the Holy Spirit is in you, he will produce more patience in your life.

TODAY'S PLAN

How can you give the Holy Spirit greater control over your life?

JOY

TODAY'S PROMISE

You will show me the way of life, granting me the joy of your presence and the pleasures of living with you forever.

—PSALM 16:11

TODAY'S THOUGHT

God does not promise that your life will always be happy. In fact, the Bible assumes problems will come your way. But God does promise lasting joy for all those who sincerely follow him. If you trust him, you have the assurance that the God of the universe loves you, wants to know you, promises to comfort and care for you, and has guaranteed your eternal future with him. This kind of joy stays with you despite your problems, and it helps you get through them without being overwhelmed.

TODAY'S PLAN

Can you tell the difference between happiness and joy?

GOALS

TODAY'S PROMISE

Sympathize with each other. Love each other as brothers and sisters. Be tenderhearted, and keep a humble attitude. Don't repay evil for evil. Don't retaliate with insults when people insult you. Instead, pay them back with a blessing. That is what God has called you to do, and he will bless you for it. —1 PETER 3:8-9

TODAY'S THOUGHT

While it's good to set big goals for family, career, or personal achievements, it's also important to set smaller daily goals. You can determine today to be kind toward others, to be humble, to respond gracefully even when someone takes advantage of you, to read your Bible, to say an encouraging word—these are small goals that bring great rewards when practiced over a lifetime. God promises to bless you for such small goals of obedience to him, for they become the essential building blocks of all the things God wants you to accomplish.

TODAY'S PLAN

What small goals can you set for yourself today?

PURPOSE

TODAY'S PROMISE

I cry out to God Most High, to God who will fulfill his purpose for me.

—PSALM 57:2

TODAY'S THOUGHT

God has both a general purpose and a specific purpose for you. In a general sense, you have been chosen by God to let the love of Jesus shine through you to make an impact on others. More specifically, God has given you unique spiritual gifts and wants you to use them to make a worthwhile contribution within your sphere of influence. The more you fulfill God's general purpose for you, the more clear your specific purpose will become.

TODAY'S PLAN

Are you fulfilling the purpose God has for you by letting Jesus' love shine through you to help others?

MIRACLES

TODAY'S PROMISE

"Yes," says the Lord, "I will do mighty miracles for you, like those I did when I rescued you from slavery in Egypt."　　　　　—MICAH 7:15

TODAY'S THOUGHT

Maybe you think a miracle is always a dramatic event, like the dead being raised back to life. But miracles are happening all around you. These supernatural occurrences may not be as dramatic as the parting of the Red Sea, but they are no less powerful. Think of the birth of a baby, the healing of an illness, the rebirth of the earth in spring, the restoration of broken relationships through the work of love and forgiveness, the salvation of sinners through faith alone, the specific call of God in your life. And these are just a few "everyday" miracles. If you think you've never seen a miracle, look closer. They are happening all around you.

TODAY'S PLAN

How can you be more open to seeing the miracles in your life?

GRACE

TODAY'S PROMISE

Sin is no longer your master, for you no longer live under the requirements of the law. Instead, you live under the freedom of God's grace. —ROMANS 6:14

TODAY'S THOUGHT

Grace is undeserved favor. It is receiving mercy when you don't expect it or deserve it. The Bible says that God extended grace to you by offering you salvation—eternal life with him—for free! You don't have to do anything to earn it. In fact, you can't earn it or buy it. You simply accept it by believing that Jesus, God's Son, died for your sins so you don't have to pay that price. God's ultimate act of grace also gives you an example of how you are to extend grace to others. You should be quick to forgive and extend kindness to others, and be generous in love—even when they don't deserve it. Grace is a tangible expression of love.

TODAY'S PLAN

How can you extend grace to someone else today?

SEARCHING

TODAY'S PROMISE

If you seek him, you will find him.

—1 CHRONICLES 28:9

TODAY'S THOUGHT

Remember that God is with you all day, every day,
so talk to him about everything that comes up at
home, at work, or in any area of your life. Share
your thoughts, needs, and concerns with him.
As you practice acknowledging his presence,
you'll begin to gain the intimacy you desire.

TODAY'S PLAN

How diligently are you searching for God?

ABANDONMENT

TODAY'S PROMISE

The LORD will not abandon his people.

—1 SAMUEL 12:22

TODAY'S THOUGHT

Even if you are suffering, it does not mean God has abandoned you. In fact, it is through suffering that you can experience God's comfort more than ever. You may feel alone in your suffering; but if God were to abandon you, he would have to stop loving you, and he cannot do that because he cannot act against his loving nature. God does not abandon you when you suffer. Rather, your compassionate God moves in to help, strengthen, and comfort you.

TODAY'S PLAN

God never gives up on you, but have you given up on God? How can you look for him at work in your life today?

POTENTIAL

TODAY'S PROMISE

You are a chosen people. You are royal priests, a holy nation, God's very own possession. As a result, you can show others the goodness of God, for he called you out of the darkness into his wonderful light.

—1 PETER 2:9

TODAY'S THOUGHT

Have you ever searched through drawers and closets for a flashlight, only to discover when you finally find it that the batteries are dead? Although the flashlight has the potential to provide light, without new batteries it is useless. You, like every believer, have within you the light of Christ and therefore the potential to shine upon others in such a way as to draw them to God. God promises that you will do amazing things if you only let him work through you.

TODAY'S PLAN

How can you let God's love shine through you more brightly?

FAITH

TODAY'S PROMISE

Faith is the confidence that what we hope for will actually happen; it gives us assurance about things we cannot see. —HEBREWS 11:1

TODAY'S THOUGHT

Faith is confident assurance that what you believe is really going to happen. When you begin to lose confidence in God, go right to his promises in the Bible. As you take confidence from the promises God has already fulfilled, you will develop greater faith that he will also fulfill his promises for the future.

TODAY'S PLAN

Are you growing more or less confident in your faith? What can you do today to develop greater confidence?

HUMILITY

TODAY'S PROMISE

He leads the humble in doing right, teaching them his way.   —PSALM 25:9

TODAY'S THOUGHT

God specifically searches out humble people in order to lead and teach them. Being humble means acknowledging your proper place before the Lord. When you worship him in humility, God will lead you and teach you the right way to live.

TODAY'S PLAN

How well do you let God lead and teach you?

DECISIONS

TODAY'S PROMISE

If you need wisdom, ask our generous God, and he will give it to you. He will not rebuke you for asking.

—JAMES 1:5

TODAY'S THOUGHT

When you are faced with a decision, you may be afraid to bother God with your problems because you think he has bigger things to worry about. But nothing could be further from the truth. God wants to help you because he loves you. He cares about your little decisions as much as your big ones. When you open the lines of communication with God, he releases his resources to you.

TODAY'S PLAN

How often do you talk to God first when you need wisdom to make a decision?

REVIVAL

TODAY'S PROMISE

The instructions of the LORD are perfect, reviving the soul. The decrees of the LORD are trustworthy, making wise the simple.

—PSALM 19:7

TODAY'S THOUGHT

Reading and meditating on God's Word revives your soul. His words are living, and therefore they are relevant to your current situation, no matter what it is. The almighty God speaks to you through the Bible, and his words bring peace, strength, comfort, wisdom, and hope— the very nourishment you need for revival. Sin starves your soul, but God's Word revives it.

TODAY'S PLAN

Are you spending enough time being revived by God's Word?

ADVERSITY

TODAY'S PROMISE

There is wonderful joy ahead, even though you have to endure many trials for a little while. These trials will show that your faith is genuine. . . . So when your faith remains strong through many trials, it will bring you much praise and glory and honor on the day when Jesus Christ is revealed to the whole world.

—1 PETER 1:6-7

TODAY'S THOUGHT

Avoiding adversity may not always be best. Though adversity may be painful at the time, it can build you up and strengthen your faith. The lives of God's people that we read about throughout the Bible testify that being faithful to God does not eliminate adversity. But these heroes of the faith also testify that adversity molds and shapes you into a stronger, better, spiritually richer person—and that is cause for joy.

TODAY'S PLAN

How can you be truly glad despite today's hard circumstances?

OPPORTUNITIES

TODAY'S PROMISE

Make the most of every opportunity in these evil days.

—EPHESIANS 5:16

We must quickly carry out the tasks assigned us by the one who sent us. The night is coming, and then no one can work.

—JOHN 9:4

TODAY'S THOUGHT

God regularly places divine appointments right in front of you—opportunities to do good, to help someone in need, or to share what you know about God. Always be on the lookout for these opportunities to give witness of your faith in words or actions. God will put the opportunities in front of you, but you need to act on them. God promises that he will make the most of your act of faith.

TODAY'S PLAN

How can you be more aware of the opportunities for witnessing that God will put in front of you today?

ENCOURAGEMENT

TODAY'S PROMISE

Don't use foul or abusive language. Let everything you say be good and helpful, so that your words will be an encouragement to those who hear them.

—EPHESIANS 4:29

TODAY'S THOUGHT

When other people encourage us, they help us regain commitment, resolve, and motivation. They inspire us with courage and hope. They help us love and live again. Encouragement is a beautiful gift, often a spiritual gift, that brings renewal. God also promises that when you encourage others, you will bring them a divine blessing as well as receive a blessing yourself.

TODAY'S PLAN

How can you encourage others more? Be ready to say something encouraging and helpful to whomever God puts in your path today.

OBEDIENCE

TODAY'S PROMISE

As a result of your ministry, they will give glory to God. For your generosity to them and to all believers will prove that you are obedient to the Good News of Christ. And they will pray for you with deep affection because of the overflowing grace God has given to you. —2 CORINTHIANS 9:13-14

TODAY'S THOUGHT

As a river flows freely through an unblocked channel, so God's grace and blessing flow through you when you follow his ways. When you obey God, your life becomes an open channel through which his love and mercy can flow to others.

TODAY'S PLAN

Is God's love and mercy freely flowing through you to the people around you?

CONSEQUENCES

TODAY'S PROMISE

You will always harvest what you plant.

—GALATIANS 6:7

TODAY'S THOUGHT

A consequence is an outcome, aftermath, or result. Some actions produce consequences that are neither morally good nor bad. For example, if you take a shower, you will get clean. But many thoughts and actions have definite good or bad consequences. Sin will always cause bad consequences. Faithfulness to God will always result in good consequences. Before you act, ask yourself, *What will the consequences of my actions be?*

TODAY'S PLAN

How often do you think about consequences before you act? Make it a practice, beginning today—it could save you loads of regret.

PRIORITIES

TODAY'S PROMISE

Wherever your treasure is, there the desires of your heart will also be.
—LUKE 12:34

TODAY'S THOUGHT

When God is at the center of your life, you will make your relationship with him your highest priority. You will long to spend time with him. You will talk to him, listen to him, think about him often, please him, and obey his Word. Your heart will yearn for him. And it's your heart that really matters to God.

TODAY'S PLAN

What does your heart truly desire? How can you make God your top priority?

POWER OF GOD

TODAY'S PROMISE

He gives power to the weak and strength to the powerless. Even youths will become weak and tired, and young men will fall in exhaustion. But those who trust in the LORD will find new strength. They will soar high on wings like eagles. They will run and not grow weary. They will walk and not faint. —ISAIAH 40:29-31

TODAY'S THOUGHT

The more you recognize your weaknesses and limitations, the more you understand God's power at work within you. Strength can make you proud and self-sufficient. That is why God often works through your weakness and your weariness, if you let him. Then there is no doubt that it is by his power—not your own—that the task is accomplished.

TODAY'S PLAN

When you are tired or frustrated by your limitations, how can you learn to eagerly anticipate God's power coming to your rescue?

HELP

TODAY'S PROMISE

The Holy Spirit helps us in our weakness. For example, we don't know what God wants us to pray for. But the Holy Spirit prays for us with groanings that cannot be expressed in words. —ROMANS 8:26

TODAY'S THOUGHT

God gives you his Holy Spirit as your personal intercessor. When you don't know what to pray, the Holy Spirit will pray for you. He will pray for you when you can't pray for yourself. God promises that you never have to worry about what to say to him. His Spirit will ask him to help you even when you don't know how to express the kind of help you need.

TODAY'S PLAN

Are you unsure how to ask God for help? Don't worry; his Holy Spirit is already helping you in exactly the way that you need it.

TIME

TODAY'S PROMISE

For everything there is a season, a time for every activity under heaven. . . . God has made everything beautiful for its own time. He has planted eternity in the human heart, but even so, people cannot see the whole scope of God's work from beginning to end. —ECCLESIASTES 3:1, 11

TODAY'S THOUGHT

The Bible is clear that time is infinite, and how you use your time on earth will have an impact on your life in heaven. So often we live by the motto "So much to do, so little time." But God does not ask you to do everything, just everything that he has called you to do. And he assures you that there is enough time to do it. The more time you invest in discovering the purpose for which God created you and living it out with obedience and responsibility, the more meaningful and significant your time on earth will be.

TODAY'S PLAN

How can you find more time to discover what God wants you to do here on earth?

HURT

TODAY'S PROMISE

We believers also groan, . . . for we long for our bodies to be released from sin and suffering. We, too, wait with eager hope for the day when God will give us our full rights as his adopted children, including the new bodies he has promised us. —ROMANS 8:23

TODAY'S THOUGHT

God does not promise believers a life free from pain and suffering. If Christians didn't hurt, other people might see God only as some sort of magician who takes away all the bad things in life. But because you have a relationship with God, he helps you, comforts you, and sometimes miraculously heals your hurt. Most important, God will one day take away all of your hurt when you arrive in heaven. Whatever pain you are experiencing is only temporary. You can be certain there is no hurt in heaven.

TODAY'S PLAN

Are you longing to be healed from hurt? Try to picture the eternity free from hurt that God promises you.

DESIRES

TODAY'S PROMISE

If you look for me wholeheartedly, you will find me.

—JEREMIAH 29:13

TODAY'S THOUGHT

Desires are good and healthy when they are directed toward that which is good and right and God-honoring. The same basic desire can be right or wrong, depending upon your motives and the object of your desire. For example, the desire to love someone is healthy and right when it is directed toward your spouse in marriage. But when that same desire is directed toward someone who is not your spouse, it is adultery. The desire to lead an organization is healthy if your motive is to serve others, but it is unhealthy and wrong if your motive is to gain power or control over others. Your greatest desire must be for a relationship with God, which will influence all your other desires.

TODAY'S PLAN

Is your greatest desire to know and love God more each day?

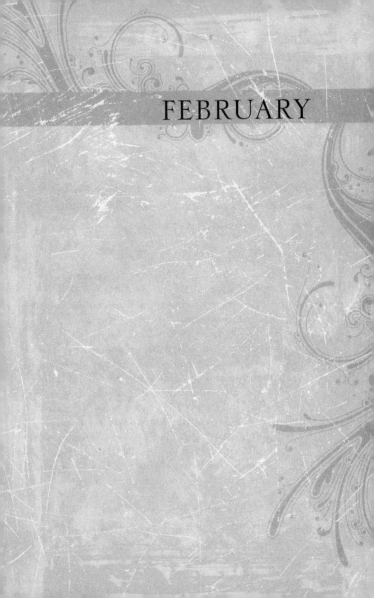

FEBRUARY

LIMITATIONS

TODAY'S PROMISE

All glory to God, who is able, through his mighty power at work within us, to accomplish infinitely more than we might ask or think. —EPHESIANS 3:20

TODAY'S THOUGHT

In God's unlimited knowledge, he created humans with limitations. He did not do this to discourage you but to help you realize your utter need for him. It is in your weakness that God's strength shines the brightest. When you accomplish something great despite your limitations, it is obvious that God was working through you and he deserves the credit. Jesus says, "What is impossible for people is possible with God" (Luke 18:27). The next time life makes you aware of your limitations, see it as an opportunity for God's power to overcome your human limitations. Eagerly anticipate how God will work through you to accomplish more than you ever could have dreamed.

TODAY'S PLAN

Which of your limitations frustrate you the most? How can you let God's power work through you in those areas of weakness?

CELEBRATION

TODAY'S PROMISE

The LORD your God . . . will take delight in you with gladness. . . . He will rejoice over you with joyful songs. —ZEPHANIAH 3:17

TODAY'S THOUGHT

God rejoices and celebrates when his people faithfully follow him and obey his commands. If you trust God's ways and follow his commands, the God of the universe will literally sing songs of joy because of you!

TODAY'S PLAN

What specific things can you do today that God can celebrate?

PEACE

TODAY'S PROMISE

Don't worry about anything; instead, pray about everything. Tell God what you need, and thank him for all he has done. Then you will experience God's peace, which exceeds anything we can understand. His peace will guard your hearts and minds as you live in Christ Jesus. —PHILIPPIANS 4:6-7

TODAY'S THOUGHT

Peace of mind comes from inviting God—the source of peace—into your life. He helps you understand that this world is only temporary. You will be able to navigate through any kind of chaos because you know God is ultimately in control. To find this harmony with God, you must ask Jesus Christ to forgive your sins and make you clean in God's sight. Then you can work toward denying your sinful desires, living a godly lifestyle, and loving others. You will begin to experience God's peace as your mind, your heart, and your actions line up with his.

TODAY'S PLAN

What can you do today to experience God's peace?

DEPRESSION

TODAY'S PROMISE

I can never escape from your Spirit! I can never get away from your presence. . . . Even in darkness I cannot hide from you. —PSALM 139:7, 12

TODAY'S THOUGHT

There is no depth you can descend to where God is not present with you. God does not regard depression as sin, nor does he take it lightly. He responds with great tenderness, understanding, and compassion to those who suffer the darkness of depression. Even if you don't feel God's presence, he has not abandoned you. You don't have to wallow in the darkness. Allow God's comforting light to enter your soul. Don't push him away. He knows everything about your situation, he knows what you are going through, and he loves you more than you could ever imagine.

TODAY'S PLAN

Even in the midst of depression, can you commit to running toward God instead of away from him?

PRAISE

TODAY'S PROMISE

It is good to give thanks to the LORD, to sing praises to the Most High. —PSALM 92:1

TODAY'S THOUGHT

When you praise the Lord, it lifts your mood. It is a deliberate act of worship that is hard to do when you are feeling down, but it produces almost immediate results. Praise the Lord for his unfailing, unconditional love for you. Praise him for the gift of salvation and eternal life. Praise him for his promise to help you through your hard times. Praise him for anything good you see around you.

TODAY'S PLAN

What can you praise God for right now?

BROKENHEARTED

TODAY'S PROMISE

The LORD is close to the brokenhearted; he rescues those whose spirits are crushed. —PSALM 34:18

TODAY'S THOUGHT

There is no quick cure for a broken heart. No pill taken twice a day for two weeks will treat it. A broken heart needs a different kind of healing. Generous doses of compassion, listening, love, comfort, encouragement, and blessing will eventually restore joy and hope to your soul. God is the master healer. Other people can help, but no one can touch your broken heart and heal it as God can. When you are hurting, move toward God, not away from him. He is the greatest source of joy and healing.

TODAY'S PLAN

In what ways can you find comfort in God's presence today?

HEART

TODAY'S PROMISE

God blesses those whose hearts are pure, for they will see God. —MATTHEW 5:8

TODAY'S THOUGHT

Doctors urge us to exercise and eat nutritious food to keep our hearts fit and healthy. In the Bible, the heart is considered to be the center of thought and feeling. It is so important that God cautions you to guard it above all else (see Proverbs 4:23) because your heart filters everything that happens to you and around you. When you neglect your heart, it becomes filthy and clogged with all kinds of foulness—bitterness, jealousy, impure thoughts. A dirty heart can no longer distinguish the good and healthy from the harmful, so it allows hurt and heartache to enter. But when you keep your heart pure and clean, it blocks the toxins of sinful thoughts and desires that could destroy you. A pure heart is the best prescription for a long, happy, and healthy life.

TODAY'S PLAN

When the Great Physician looks at your heart, in what condition will he find it?

ANGER

TODAY'S PROMISE

His anger lasts only a moment, but his favor lasts a lifetime! Weeping may last through the night, but joy comes with the morning. —PSALM 30:5

TODAY'S THOUGHT

The Bible promises that God is kind and merciful and will always be ready to receive you with love when you confess your sin and seek a relationship with him. One of the worst caricatures of God is the image of him as an angry old man. Instead of fierce anger and punishment, God corrects his children with gentle discipline that is actually an expression of his love in action.

TODAY'S PLAN

What are some ways you can see God's merciful love in action in your life today?

KINDNESS

TODAY'S PROMISE

If you give even a cup of cold water to one of the least of my followers, you will surely be rewarded.

—MATTHEW 10:42

TODAY'S THOUGHT

God rewards kindness because it demonstrates unconditional love, the supreme character trait of a Christian. True kindness is not a single random act but a lifestyle. Begin by showing kindness in the little things you do and say, and strive to be truly kind in all situations. Kindness should not be motivated by the promise of reward, but God promises that you will be rewarded for your kindness.

TODAY'S PLAN

What small act of kindness can you do for someone today? How can you show kindness to someone you don't know, or even to someone you don't like?

LOVE

TODAY'S PROMISE

Don't just pretend to love others. Really love them.

—ROMANS 12:9

TODAY'S THOUGHT

It's easy to like people who are likable, but you model God's love more when you show love to those who are unlovable. There are no perfect people—even among Christians. But you can take joy in reaching out to and loving those imperfect people God has placed in your sphere of influence. You may be surprised at how God can bring the most unlikely individuals together as friends. When you reach out to others in love, your heart will be changed.

TODAY'S PLAN

Who in your life is difficult to love? How can you show love for that person anyway?

GENEROSITY

TODAY'S PROMISE

Wherever your treasure is, there the desires of your heart will also be. —MATTHEW 6:21

TODAY'S THOUGHT

Who is more generous—a billionaire who gives one million dollars to the church, or a struggling single mom who gives only a hundred? If you do have a lot of money, does that mean you are not generous? Jesus says we can't know the answers to these questions without knowing the heart of the giver. The Bible shows us that God doesn't focus on how much money you have but rather on how generous you are with it. One thing is clear: What you spend your money on reveals what you care most about. When you realize that everything you have is a gift from a generous God, it motivates you to share your money and possessions more freely.

TODAY'S PLAN

How might your generous giving impact the lives of those around you?

OBEDIENCE

TODAY'S PROMISE

If someone claims, "I know God," but doesn't obey God's commandments, that person is . . . not living in the truth. But those who obey God's word truly show how completely they love him. That is how we know we are living in him. —1 John 2:4-5

TODAY'S THOUGHT

Do you want to show how much you love God? He tells you how—simply obey him. And how do you do that? He tells you how—follow his commandments in the Bible, which is his instruction manual for living well and loving others. When you obey God, you demonstrate your belief that what he says is true. The more you obey him, the more you will see that following God's Word really is best. You will begin to experience the blessings of obedience, and you will love God even more for showing you how to live a life of joy and fulfillment.

TODAY'S PLAN

How well are you obeying God? How does it affect your love for him?

LOYALTY

TODAY'S PROMISE

The LORD leads with unfailing love and faithfulness all who keep his covenant and obey his demands.
—PSALM 25:10

TODAY'S THOUGHT

Loyalty can be defined as a highly personal form of commitment. Loyalty says, "No matter what happens around us or between us, there is no fear, doubt, or hurt that can make me turn my back on you." When you have loyalty in a relationship, it is secure and solid. When you do not, you live in insecurity and fear. The Bible teaches that loyalty is part of the very character of God. He expresses his loyalty by refusing to give up on you no matter how often you disappoint him with your sin. You express your loyalty to God by obeying his Word.

TODAY'S PLAN

How are you showing your loyalty to God? How can you model the same loyalty to your loved ones?

LOVE

TODAY'S PROMISE

Love is patient and kind. Love is not jealous or boastful or proud or rude. It does not demand its own way. It is not irritable, and it keeps no record of being wronged. It does not rejoice about injustice but rejoices whenever the truth wins out. Love never gives up, never loses faith, is always hopeful, and endures through every circumstance.

—1 CORINTHIANS 13:4-7

TODAY'S THOUGHT

These well-known verses are some of the most eloquent and accurate descriptions of love ever written. Contrary to popular opinion, true love is first of all a courageous commitment and an unwavering choice to care for another person. Then love in turn produces powerful feelings. When you practice the qualities and behaviors described in these verses, the Bible promises you will experience satisfaction and fulfillment.

TODAY'S PLAN

Is your love for others based first on commitment or on feelings?

LOVE

TODAY'S PROMISE

This is real love—not that we loved God, but that he loved us and sent his Son as a sacrifice to take away our sins.

—1 JOHN 4:10

TODAY'S THOUGHT

The statement "God is love" means that God is the only source of love and only he could create us with the ability to love. Therefore, no one knows as much about love as God does. Intimacy with God means experiencing his love to the fullest and showing that love to him in return. The love he communicates is completely loyal, trusting, serving, and revealing. God created marriage to illustrate what an intimate relationship with him should look like. Therefore, a husband and wife should strive to be completely loyal, vulnerable, caring, honest, loving, and trustworthy.

TODAY'S PLAN

Do you have an intimate relationship with God? If you are married, how can you experience that kind of intimacy with your spouse?

CHURCH

TODAY'S PROMISE

Where two or three gather together as my followers, I am there among them. —MATTHEW 18:20

TODAY'S THOUGHT

God lives in the heart of every believer, but he also lives within the community of the church. When the church is gathered together, God meets his people in a special way. Just as being present at a live concert or sports event makes it much more exciting, participating with other believers in worshiping God makes it much more meaningful.

TODAY'S PLAN

How can you experience God more deeply with other believers?

PURSUIT BY GOD

TODAY'S PROMISE

"When that day comes," says the LORD, ". . . I will be faithful to you and make you mine, and you will finally know me as the LORD. . . . I will show love to those I called 'Not loved.' And to those I called 'Not my people,' I will say, 'Now you are my people.' And they will reply, 'You are our God!'"

—HOSEA 2:16, 20, 23

TODAY'S THOUGHT

God wants a personal relationship with each person he has created. He pursues you, not to get something from you but to give something wonderful to you—help, hope, power, salvation, joy, peace, eternal life. God pursues you because he knows that only he can transform your life forever.

TODAY'S PLAN

Are you still running from God's love, or have you surrendered to his pursuing?

FRIENDSHIP

TODAY'S PROMISE

Since our friendship with God was restored by the death of his Son while we were still his enemies, we will certainly be saved through the life of his Son. So now we can rejoice in our wonderful new relationship with God because our Lord Jesus Christ has made us friends of God.
—ROMANS 5:10-11

TODAY'S THOUGHT

The God of the universe promises that you can be his friend. You simply have to want to. Unfortunately, many of us don't. True friends hold each other accountable and do whatever they can to please each other. Many people don't want to live the kind of life that pleases God. They don't realize that pleasing God gives life true meaning and joy. God created us to be in relationships, especially in a relationship with him through faith in Jesus Christ. As you develop your relationship with God, you develop a friendship with him. He is your Lord, but he also desires to be your friend.

TODAY'S PLAN

Do you see yourself as a friend of God?

TRUST

TODAY'S PROMISE

No, I will not break my covenant; I will not take back a single word I said. I have sworn an oath to David, and in my holiness I cannot lie.

—PSALM 89:34-35

TODAY'S THOUGHT

We trust only those who can be counted on to always tell the truth and keep their promises. God is the source of truth; he cannot lie. Therefore, everything he says in his Word, the Bible, is true. All of it must be true, or else we could not fully trust God. As you read the Bible, find God's promises to you. Discover how much he loves you and wants a close relationship with you. When you trust him with your whole heart, he will make himself known to you in amazing and powerful ways. Then you will experience a breakthrough in your relationship with God.

TODAY'S PLAN

Do you trust that everything God says is true? How can you develop greater faith in God's truth?

SPIRITUAL WARFARE

TODAY'S PROMISE

Put on every piece of God's armor so you will be able to resist the enemy in the time of evil. Then after the battle you will still be standing firm. —EPHESIANS 6:13

TODAY'S THOUGHT

Satan always strikes at your weak spots, those areas you refuse to give over to God. These weaknesses are the joints in your spiritual armor at which the enemy takes aim. In those areas of weakness, God promises to give you the strength to overcome the attacks of sin and Satan. But you must ask God to cover your weaknesses with his strength.

TODAY'S PLAN

In what area are you most vulnerable to spiritual attack?

ADDICTION

TODAY'S PROMISE

The Holy Spirit produces this kind of fruit in our lives: love, joy, peace, patience, kindness, goodness, faithfulness, gentleness, and self-control.

—GALATIANS 5:22-23

TODAY'S THOUGHT

We all have our addictions, whether they are simply bad habits or serious dependencies. One thing all of us are dangerously addicted to is sin. We consistently—daily—disobey God's Word through sinful thoughts, words, or actions. The only cure is to submit to the control of God and his Holy Spirit. When you are under God's control, the Holy Spirit replaces the destructive things in your life with good things. God's transforming power is the only thing that can ultimately heal you of all addictions.

TODAY'S PLAN

What is some fruit of the Spirit you can cultivate today to help break your sin addiction?

INTEGRITY

TODAY'S PROMISE

If you are faithful in little things, you will be faithful in large ones. But if you are dishonest in little things, you won't be honest with greater responsibilities. —LUKE 16:10

TODAY'S THOUGHT

Integrity is essentially the correspondence between your character and the character of God. To develop integrity, your character must become more and more like God's. Just as pure gold is the result of a refining process that purifies the metal and tests it with fire, a life of integrity is the result of a refining process in which you are tested daily to see how pure you are. If God sees that your thoughts and actions are becoming increasingly pure through this testing, then your character is becoming more like his, and you are gradually gaining integrity.

TODAY'S PLAN

Is your character becoming more or less like God's each day?

CHARACTER

TODAY'S PROMISE

Dear brothers and sisters, when troubles come your way, consider it an opportunity for great joy. For you know that when your faith is tested, your endurance has a chance to grow. So let it grow, for when your endurance is fully developed, you will be perfect and complete, needing nothing. —JAMES 1:2-4

TODAY'S THOUGHT

It may seem to be a contradiction, but adversity actually produces strength. Just as your muscles grow only when pushed beyond their limits, your character grows only when the pressures of life push against it and test its strength. Developing a strong character takes time and constant attention. Your character will get soft if you stop working on it. Only through hard work will you achieve great accomplishment and the satisfaction that goes with it. Pain, trials, and temptations refine us so that over time we are better equipped to deal with them.

TODAY'S PLAN

How might some of the problems you have today be building your character?

MATURITY

TODAY'S PROMISE

Let your roots grow down into him, and let your lives be built on him. Then your faith will grow strong in the truth you were taught, and you will overflow with thankfulness.
—COLOSSIANS 2:7

TODAY'S THOUGHT

Spiritual growth is like physical growth—you start small and grow one day at a time. As you grow, however, you need more nourishment. You get spiritual nourishment by challenging your mind in the study of God's Word, asking questions about it, and seeking answers through prayer and the counsel and experience of other believers. Look at each day as a stepping-stone, and before you know it, you will be on your way to spiritual maturity.

TODAY'S PLAN

What small step can you take today toward spiritual maturity?

HONESTY

TODAY'S PROMISE

Truthful words stand the test of time, but lies are soon exposed.
—PROVERBS 12:19

TODAY'S THOUGHT

Lies are usually exposed because even the dishonest don't like to be deceived. Dishonesty can ruin your reputation. It can make you untrustworthy and cause you to lose your friends, your spouse, your home, or your job. It can even land you in jail. Ultimately, a lifestyle of dishonesty pits you against the God of truth, who doesn't allow dishonest people into his eternal Kingdom. That is why practicing honesty is so important.

TODAY'S PLAN

How are you tempted to be dishonest in your everyday life? What are some ways you can be honest in those situations instead?

OVERWHELMED

TODAY'S PROMISE

Don't be afraid, for I am with you. Don't be discouraged, for I am your God. I will strengthen you and help you. I will hold you up with my victorious right hand. —ISAIAH 41:10

As soon as I pray, you answer me; you encourage me by giving me strength. —PSALM 138:3

TODAY'S THOUGHT

It's easy to become overwhelmed by the challenges and struggles we must face each day. But when you begin to see the obstacles in your life as opportunities for God to show you his strength, they will not seem so overwhelming. The hardships and worries that frighten you may be the tools God will use to make you stronger and to equip you to fight life's battles. The mystery and miracle of prayer also allow God to work in your situation and give you his strength.

TODAY'S PLAN

How have you seen God work through overwhelming situations in the past?

CONTENTMENT

TODAY'S PROMISE

By his divine power, God has given us everything we need for living a godly life. We have received all of this by coming to know him, the one who called us to himself by means of his marvelous glory and excellence.

—2 PETER 1:3

TODAY'S THOUGHT

When your contentment depends on things going your way, you will become unhappy when they don't. When your contentment comes from watching Jesus meet your needs, you will be secure and happy because you will have all you need. You will know that God's plan for you, which is always best, is working out. He will teach you to discern the valuable things in life from the distractions.

TODAY'S PLAN

How can you learn to find greater contentment in the things God has already given you?

POWER OF GOD

TODAY'S PROMISE

God is awesome in his sanctuary. The God of Israel gives power and strength to his people. Praise be to God!

—PSALM 68:35

TODAY'S THOUGHT

The God who created the world and who defeats Satan promises to offer his power to you. If you believe that God sent Jesus Christ to save you from sin, and if you ask him to forgive your sin and remove it, he will replace the power of sin over your heart with the power to do good, to accomplish great things, and to resist the forces of evil. Then you will be able to use God's power for godly purposes.

TODAY'S PLAN

How can you tap into the power of God today?

MEANING

My life is worth nothing to me unless I use it for finishing the work assigned me by the Lord Jesus.

—ACTS 20:24

I take joy in doing your will, my God, for your instructions are written on my heart. —PSALM 40:8

TODAY'S THOUGHT

You don't need to do earthshaking things in order to have a meaningful life. Your life has meaning when you do the work that God has given you to do. Whether you are changing diapers, running a company, or evangelizing the world, do it as though God is working through you—because he is! Your life has meaning because you are sharing the love of God with everyone in your circle of influence.

TODAY'S PLAN

How can you find greater meaning in your daily tasks?

MARCH

PROMISES OF GOD

TODAY'S PROMISE

God has given both his promise and his oath. These two things are unchangeable because it is impossible for God to lie. Therefore, we who have fled to him for refuge can have great confidence as we hold to the hope that lies before us.

—HEBREWS 6:18

TODAY'S THOUGHT

A wedding is one of the most sacred of ceremonies. The vows that a husband and wife take as they enter into marriage are breathtaking in beauty and boldness, and they are intended to be binding "as long as you both shall live." Yet divorce statistics prove that even the most serious of human promises is not taken very seriously today. Not so with God. God's promises are anchored in his unchanging character and his steadfast love. In fact, God has never broken a promise. Can we expect anything less from the One who cannot lie?

TODAY'S PLAN

Do you know anyone who carries through on every promise? Look to God's Word and take comfort in his perfect record of keeping promises.

JEALOUSY

TODAY'S PROMISE

Don't envy sinners, but always continue to fear the Lord. You will be rewarded for this; your hope will not be disappointed. —PROVERBS 23:17-18

TODAY'S THOUGHT

Jealousy eats away at you. It causes you to focus on destructive emotions such as greed and bitterness rather than on healthy emotions such as content- ment with what you have and genuine happiness over the success of others.

TODAY'S PLAN

Is there someone you envy? Begin praying for that person every day, and see how your envy is transformed into joy.

FAILURE

TODAY'S PROMISE

*Each time [God] said, "My grace is all you need.
My power works best in weakness." So now I am
glad to boast about my weaknesses, so that the power
of Christ can work through me.* —2 CORINTHIANS 12:9

TODAY'S THOUGHT

One thing is certain: You must learn to live
with failure. Everyone has weaknesses. Everyone
fails—a lot. Strong character depends not on
how often you fail but on how you respond to
failure. Adam and Eve, for example, responded
to failure by trying to blame each other rather
than admitting their mistakes and seeking forgiveness. The apostle Paul, however, learned to
appreciate his weaknesses and failures because
God was working through them. Those who
admit their failures and learn from them
will go on to accomplish great things.

TODAY'S PLAN

How can you learn to respond better to failure?

REST

TODAY'S PROMISE

Jesus said, "Come to me, all of you who are weary and carry heavy burdens, and I will give you rest. Take my yoke upon you. Let me teach you, because I am humble and gentle at heart, and you will find rest for your souls. For my yoke is easy to bear, and the burden I give you is light."

—MATTHEW 11:28-30

TODAY'S THOUGHT

When you visit friends who live far away and you spend the night with them, usually they've prepared a room for you to make you comfortable and help you rest. God does the same for you. When you come to him, he has already prepared a place where you can feel safe and you can rest quietly. In his presence, the burdens of the world are put into perspective. When you need spiritual rest and refreshment, go to the Creator of rest and linger with him. Only the Creator can give you recreation.

TODAY'S PLAN

How can you find a quiet place to rest with God today?

ACCEPTANCE

TODAY'S PROMISE

Accept each other just as Christ has accepted you so that God will be given glory. —ROMANS 15:7

TODAY'S THOUGHT

The way you treat other people can greatly influence them—for better or worse. Use your influence positively and accept others for who they are. Don't be quick to judge. Don't accept only those people who are like you or who are important or who are popular. Welcome everyone in the way Jesus would welcome them. It isn't a matter of searching for the best people to be around; it's a matter of bringing out the best in the people God has brought to you. Then God will be glorified because you will recognize that the way he treats people brings out the best in everyone.

TODAY'S PLAN

Do you know someone who is struggling to be accepted? What can you do to affirm that person and help others accept him or her as well?

CONFESSION

TODAY'S PROMISE

If my people who are called by my name will humble themselves and pray and seek my face and turn from their wicked ways, I will hear from heaven and will forgive their sins and restore their land.

—2 CHRONICLES 7:14

TODAY'S THOUGHT

Confession is admitting your sins to God so he can forgive you. Sin separates you from God; confession indicates your desire to restore your relationship with him. When you confess your sin, you agree that something is wrong and needs to be made right, that your damaged relationships with God and with others need to be repaired.

TODAY'S PLAN

When was the last time you confessed your sin to God? Do it today, using this simple, ancient prayer of the church: "Lord Jesus Christ, Son of God, have mercy upon me, a sinner."

BROKENNESS

TODAY'S PROMISE

He heals the brokenhearted and bandages their wounds.
—PSALM 147:3

TODAY'S THOUGHT

Picture God personally tending to your wounds—the physical hurts of your body and the emotional blows to your soul. Imagine the tender touch of the Great Physician as he heals your brokenness. When God performs his healing in your life, you will find joy, and others will rejoice with you.

TODAY'S PLAN

Where do you need healing today? Will you allow God to touch you in your brokenness?

NEEDS

TODAY'S PROMISE

Your heavenly Father already knows all your needs. Seek the Kingdom of God above all else, and live righteously, and he will give you everything you need.
— MATTHEW 6:32-33

TODAY'S THOUGHT

The Bible promises that God will supply all of your needs. The problem comes when your definition of your needs is different from God's. The first thing you must do is study his Word to discover what God says you need for a fulfilling life.

TODAY'S PLAN

What are some things you think you need? Are they the things God says you need?

PERSEVERANCE

TODAY'S PROMISE

God blesses those who patiently endure testing and temptation. Afterward they will receive the crown of life that God has promised to those who love him.

—JAMES 1:12

TODAY'S THOUGHT

Perseverance has been appropriately defined as "courage stretched out." Although God sometimes delivers you from difficult or painful circumstances, he often calls you to a courageous and enduring faithfulness in the midst of trials. According to the Bible, perseverance is not only enduring situations of suffering but overcoming them with patience, hope, and joy. When you persevere, God promises to reward you.

TODAY'S PLAN

What might your future look like if you were to endure today's problems with patience and hope?

FEAR

TODAY'S PROMISE

The LORD is my light and my salvation—so why should I be afraid? The LORD is my fortress, protecting me from danger, so why should I tremble?

—PSALM 27:1

TODAY'S THOUGHT

Fear turns your focus away from God and toward the troubles that intimidate you. Look at your fears as opportunities to rely on God for his help, his guidance, and his saving power. No problem is too big for the God who promises to save and protect you.

TODAY'S PLAN

What are you afraid of? How can a heavenly perspective help you overcome those fears?

FAITHFULNESS

TODAY'S PROMISE

If we are unfaithful, he remains faithful, for he cannot deny who he is.
—2 TIMOTHY 2:13

TODAY'S THOUGHT

Who are you really—deep down inside? Do you really love others? Are you really faithful to your family and friends? Faithfulness is necessary for maintaining love because even those closest to you will disappoint you at times. In the same way, you have disappointed God. But despite your unfaithfulness, God loves you and remains faithful to you. Model that same love of Christ to others, and remain faithful to them even when they fail you. Your faithfulness will show that your love is genuine.

TODAY'S PLAN

How can you show greater faithfulness to your loved ones and to God?

COURAGE

TODAY'S PROMISE

Don't be afraid, for I am with you. Don't be discouraged, for I am your God. I will strengthen you and help you. I will hold you up with my victorious right hand. —ISAIAH 41:10

TODAY'S THOUGHT

To experience fear is normal. To be paralyzed by fear, however, can be an indication that you doubt God's promises or his ability to care for you in the face of danger. Realize that courage doesn't come from your qualifications or your credentials but from the promise of God's presence and power. When you know God is with you and helping you, you can face any fear.

TODAY'S PLAN

Are you paralyzed by fear? How can God's promises give you the courage to face your fears?

NEGLECT

TODAY'S PROMISE

We must listen very carefully to the truth we have heard, or we may drift away from it. —HEBREWS 2:1

TODAY'S THOUGHT

A child who is neglected longs for the love of a parent and often suffers extreme emotional trauma because they do not receive it. A friend who is neglected soon drifts away, and a spouse who is neglected eventually becomes despondent and lonely. It is just as tragic when you neglect your heavenly Father. God patiently, persistently, and lovingly extends his arms to you each day. How often do you ignore his overtures? Don't neglect your most important relationship.

TODAY'S PLAN

How can you begin today to restore any relationships you have neglected?

GUIDANCE

TODAY'S PROMISE

Your word is a lamp to guide my feet and a light for my path.
—PSALM 119:105

TODAY'S THOUGHT

God's guidance is not so much like a searchlight that brightens a large area as it is like a flashlight that illuminates just enough of the path ahead to show you where to take the next few steps. God has a definite plan for you—never doubt that. But usually he doesn't reveal it all at once. He wants you to learn to trust him each step of the way.

TODAY'S PLAN

In what one area of your life can you trust God's guidance by taking just a few steps forward today?

COMMITMENT

TODAY'S PROMISE

Commit everything you do to the LORD. Trust him, and he will help you.

—PSALM 37:5

TODAY'S THOUGHT

Being committed to God means that you trust him to lead you and do what is best for you. It means resolving to do your best to obey all of God's Word in all areas of your life. As a human being with a sinful nature, you will never be able to achieve such a high goal in this life, but that should not stop you from trying to do your best. When you commit to following God, he commits to leading you.

TODAY'S PLAN

How can you live out a stronger commitment to God?

PRAYER

TODAY'S PROMISE

The LORD is close to all who call on him, yes, to all who call on him in truth. —PSALM 145:18

TODAY'S THOUGHT

Prayer is an intimate conversation with your heavenly Father. Through prayer he makes his love and resources available to you. Just as you enjoy being with the people you love, you will learn to enjoy spending time with God the more you get to know him and understand how much he loves you. Good conversation includes listening as well as talking, so be sure to make time for God to speak to you. When you listen to God, he will make his wisdom and his will known to you.

TODAY'S PLAN

Do you feel close to God when you pray?

EMOTIONS

TODAY'S PROMISE

Guard your heart above all else, for it determines the course of your life.

—PROVERBS 4:23

TODAY'S THOUGHT

The Bible says that "the human heart is the most deceitful of all things, and desperately wicked" (Jeremiah 17:9). It is the center of the battle between your sinful nature and your new nature in Christ. The heart is also the center of your emotions; your emotions are constantly influenced by your sinful nature. This should make you cautious about trusting your feelings. Guarding your heart means not allowing the influences of sin and Satan to touch your emotional life. If you look at pornography, the good and right emotions of love and respect turn into lust and convince you to enjoy those sinful pleasures. To effectively guard your heart, you must fill it with God's Word. God's words come from his heart, which is good and perfect.

TODAY'S PLAN

Have your emotions lately been influenced more by your sinful nature or by God's Word?

PAIN

TODAY'S PROMISE

In his kindness God called you to share in his eternal glory by means of Christ Jesus. So after you have suffered a little while, he will restore, support, and strengthen you, and he will place you on a firm foundation.
—1 PETER 5:10

TODAY'S THOUGHT

When you accidentally cut yourself, you immediately focus on how to stop the bleeding and ease the pain. Sometimes when you feel as if God has abandoned you, it is because you have become so focused on easing your pain that you have neglected God. Perhaps you have forgotten that he has promised to help you in your difficulties. God will never desert those who follow him. He doesn't take the day off and forget about you or your pain. Even if you must experience pain for a time, remember that God promises to help and heal you.

TODAY'S PLAN

Has the pain of difficult circumstances taken your focus off of God and his promises?

ACCEPTANCE

TODAY'S PROMISE

If you confess with your mouth that Jesus is Lord and believe in your heart that God raised him from the dead, you will be saved. For it is by believing in your heart that you are made right with God, and it is by confessing with your mouth that you are saved.

—ROMANS 10:9-10

TODAY'S THOUGHT

There is a big difference between being loved by God for who you are and being accepted into heaven. If you are convicted of a crime, you must suffer the consequences no matter how much you are loved. All people are guilty of sinning against God. Jesus suffered the consequences for your sin, but you must believe and accept that he did. Your sin separates you from a holy and perfect God. But your faith in Jesus makes you holy and acceptable in God's sight, and it will reunite you with him in heaven.

TODAY'S PLAN

Have you accepted Jesus' offer of forgiveness so that you can be accepted into heaven?

HUMILITY

TODAY'S PROMISE

Anyone who becomes as humble as this little child is the greatest in the Kingdom of Heaven.

—MATTHEW 18:4

TODAY'S THOUGHT

The less you strive to bring honor to yourself, the more God will honor and bless you. Pride builds barriers that keep God out of your life. Humility opens the way for God to work in your life because you are willing to seek his help and give him the honor. Humility is true strength, for its effects reach into the Kingdom of Heaven. Pride is true weakness, for it reaches no further than your own ego.

TODAY'S PLAN

In what way is a child humble? How can you develop such humility?

FASTING

TODAY'S PROMISE

When you fast, don't make it obvious, as the hypocrites do, for they try to look miserable and disheveled so people will admire them for their fasting. . . . When you fast, comb your hair and wash your face. Then no one will notice that you are fasting, except your Father. . . . And your Father, who sees everything, will reward you. —MATTHEW 6:16-18

TODAY'S THOUGHT

Fasting is abstaining from things that you regularly enjoy in order to give greater attention to spiritual concerns. It is one of the most frequently illustrated spiritual exercises in Scripture. Fasting has been described as praying with the body. God promises that when you fast, you will be rewarded. It is a significant way to develop spiritual power and a more immediate sense of God's presence.

TODAY'S PLAN

If you fast, look at it as improving your communication with God rather than giving up something.

HEAVEN

TODAY'S PROMISE

And then at last, the sign that the Son of Man is coming will appear in the heavens, and there will be deep mourning among all the peoples of the earth. And they will see the Son of Man coming on the clouds of heaven with power and great glory. And he will send out his angels with the mighty blast of a trumpet, and they will gather his chosen ones from all over the world—from the farthest ends of the earth and heaven. —MATTHEW 24:30-31

TODAY'S THOUGHT

One of the greatest promises in the Bible is that Jesus will come again. He will come to judge—righting all wrong and vindicating his followers. And he will come to forgive—pardoning all who believe in him as Lord. All who believe will be gathered together with him in heaven and will live there forever.

TODAY'S PLAN

If Jesus comes back today, will you be ready for him?

DEATH

TODAY'S PROMISE

I am the resurrection and the life. Anyone who believes in me will live, even after dying. Everyone who lives in me and believes in me will never ever die.

—JOHN 11:25-26

TODAY'S THOUGHT

Why are we so afraid to die? Often it is because we are uncertain about what happens after death. This life is all we know; death represents the unknown. When you die physically, you leave your earthly body and your place in the earthly community. But if you die spiritually, you will miss eternal life in heaven with God and with his people; you will be separated from God forever. When Christians die physically, they continue to live spiritually as they take up residence in heaven. If you believe Jesus is your Savior, death is not the end but only the beginning of an eternity of unspeakable joy in the Lord's presence.

TODAY'S PLAN

How can you look at death as the beginning rather than the end?

PRODUCTIVITY

TODAY'S PROMISE

Oh, the joys of those who do not follow the advice of the wicked, or stand around with sinners, or join in with mockers. But they delight in the law of the LORD, meditating on it day and night. They are like trees planted along the riverbank, bearing fruit each season. Their leaves never wither, and they prosper in all they do. —PSALM 1:1-3

TODAY'S THOUGHT

The Bible often uses metaphors of trees and vines to paint a picture of how people should be useful and productive. As a follower of God, you are to live a life that bears the fruit of righteousness, justice, kindness, love, and truth. These are the important and productive means of growing the Kingdom of God on earth. When you cultivate this kind of productivity, others will be drawn to the beauty of God and his way of living.

TODAY'S PLAN

How can you be more productive for the Kingdom of God today?

HEALING

TODAY'S PROMISE

He will wipe every tear from their eyes, and there will be no more death or sorrow or crying or pain. All these things are gone forever.　　　—REVELATION 21:4

TODAY'S THOUGHT

Jesus has the ability and the desire to heal you. When you pray for healing, you are expressing your faith and trust in him. Although he doesn't heal all of your illnesses, griefs, or hurts in this life, he performs a great miracle in you every day when he heals your soul from sin. And he promises that one day you will be fully healed and perfect with him.

TODAY'S PLAN

What kind of healing do you need from God?

FAITH

TODAY'S PROMISE

Believe in the Lord Jesus and you will be saved.

—ACTS 16:31

TODAY'S THOUGHT

Faith is more than just believing; it is entrusting your very life to what you believe. For example, you may *believe* that someone can cross a deep gorge on a tightrope. But would you *trust* that person to carry you across? If you truly had faith, you would say yes. Faith in God means that you are willing to trust him with your whole life. You are willing to follow his guidelines for living, as outlined in the Bible, because you have the conviction that his will is best for you. You are even willing to endure ridicule and persecution for your faith because you are sure that God is who he says he is and he will keep his promises about salvation and eternal life in heaven.

TODAY'S PLAN

How strong is your faith?

DIGNITY

TODAY'S PROMISE

You made [human beings] only a little lower than God and crowned them with glory and honor.

—PSALM 8:5

TODAY'S THOUGHT

To have dignity means to understand who God made you to be—a human being who bears his image. In the eyes of the Creator, you have great worth and value, and you have been made for a special purpose. Your dignity comes not from what others think about you but from God himself. God chose to create you, and he gave you unique gifts and abilities. Not only does this give you dignity, it gives you the confidence to boldly serve him wherever he leads you.

TODAY'S PLAN

How can your God-given sense of dignity give you confidence and purpose today?

SALVATION

TODAY'S PROMISE

The wages of sin is death, but the free gift of God is eternal life through Christ Jesus our Lord.

—ROMANS 6:23

TODAY'S THOUGHT

God promises salvation to everyone who accepts it. When you confess your sins and are sorry for them, and when you believe that Jesus died for your sins, you will be saved from the punishment you deserve. God looks at you as though you have never sinned, and he gives you eternal life in heaven.

TODAY'S PLAN

Have you accepted God's free gift of eternal life in heaven?

BALANCE

TODAY'S PROMISE

Don't copy the behavior and customs of this world, but let God transform you into a new person by changing the way you think. Then you will learn to know God's will for you, which is good and pleasing and perfect.

—ROMANS 12:2

TODAY'S THOUGHT

Jesus modeled a life of balance between socializing and solitariness, action and reflection, mission and meditation, hard work and rest for spiritual reenergizing. This pace allowed him to be guided by God's will instead of human pressures. When you live a balanced life, you realize that every need and every opportunity are not necessarily the things God is calling you to do. When you let God change your thinking to reflect his thinking, he will show you what to do and what not to do. Then you can live according to his priorities and his will.

TODAY'S PLAN

How can you achieve balance between what you want to do and what God wants you to do?

HEAVEN

TODAY'S PROMISE

We are looking forward to the new heavens and new earth he has promised, a world filled with God's righteousness. —2 PETER 3:13

TODAY'S THOUGHT

God originally created earth to be heaven—the place where he would live side by side with humankind and walk and talk with them. Sin changed all that. It separated us from God and corrupted the earth. But God's original plan for a heavenly paradise that is a very physical place—with trees and plants, mountains and waterfalls, fruits and vegetables—will still be accomplished someday. The Bible refers to this as the new earth—the place where we will be reunited with God. The new earth where we will live forever with God will be very similar to the earth we live on now. God said that the earth he created was "very good," so we can be sure that the new earth he is preparing for us will be familiar but even better.

TODAY'S PLAN

What are some ideas you have about heaven that might actually be misconceptions?

EQUALITY

TODAY'S PROMISE

Remember that the heavenly Father to whom you pray has no favorites. He will judge or reward you according to what you do. So you must live in reverent fear of him during your time as "foreigners in the land."

—1 PETER 1:17

TODAY'S THOUGHT

Doing good deeds doesn't get you into heaven; faith in Jesus does. That's equally true for everyone. God does promise, however, that your good deeds here on earth will bring rewards in heaven. You may not know what those rewards will be, but you can be sure they will be wonderful and are worth working toward. God doesn't play favorites. You have just as much opportunity as everyone else to do good deeds that will bring you heavenly rewards.

TODAY'S PLAN

How can you go out of your way today to do something good for someone who isn't expecting it?

APRIL

MISTAKES

TODAY'S PROMISE

"Why are you so angry?" the LORD asked Cain. . . . "You will be accepted if you do what is right. But if you refuse to do what is right, then watch out! Sin is crouching at the door, eager to control you."

—GENESIS 4:6-7

TODAY'S THOUGHT

If you burn your toast at breakfast, the mistake has no lasting consequences. But if a doctor misreads someone's chart and removes a kidney instead of the appendix, the doctor has made a mistake with considerably greater implications. We usually think of making a mistake as doing something wrong by accident. That is often the case, but a mistake can also be intentional and sinful—like turning away from God. If you have made that mistake, correct it before it's too late!

TODAY'S PLAN

What is the worst mistake you've ever made? Have you allowed God to fix and forgive it?

FORGIVENESS

TODAY'S PROMISE

If you forgive those who sin against you, your heavenly Father will forgive you. But if you refuse to forgive others, your Father will not forgive your sins.

—MATTHEW 6:14–15

TODAY'S THOUGHT

If you are unwilling to forgive others, it shows that you have not understood or benefited from God's forgiveness, because forgiveness is motivated by unconditional love. When God forgives you, you are freed from guilt and restored to fellowship with him. When you forgive someone who has wronged you, you are freed from bitterness and resentment so you can rebuild your relationship with that person. And when someone else forgives you, you are freed from guilt and indebtedness to them. Receiving forgiveness from God, forgiving others, and being forgiven by others are at the heart of what it means to be a Christian.

TODAY'S PLAN

Do you need to forgive someone who has wronged you?

JESUS

TODAY'S PROMISE

*Jesus Christ, the Son of God, does not waver
between "Yes" and "No." . . . As God's ultimate
"Yes," he always does what he says. For all of
God's promises have been fulfilled in Christ with
a resounding "Yes!" And through Christ, our
"Amen" (which means "Yes") ascends to God
for his glory.*

—2 CORINTHIANS 1:19-20

TODAY'S THOUGHT

Jesus Christ is the Son of God, the Savior who
was promised by God. He was fully God and fully
human. He lived a sinless life so that he could
die on the cross to take the punishment that you
deserve for your sins. Then he rose from the
dead to prove that he has power over death
and to assure you that if you believe in him
as Lord, you will also be raised to eternal life.
God promises that when you believe in Jesus,
you will live forever in heaven with him.

TODAY'S PLAN

*Do you believe God's promises about Jesus? If not,
what would it take for you to believe?*

ASSURANCE

TODAY'S PROMISE

If we are faithful to the end, trusting God just as firmly as when we first believed, we will share in all that belongs to Christ.
—HEBREWS 3:14

TODAY'S THOUGHT

If you believe that Jesus died on the cross to save you, if you confess your sins to him, and if you acknowledge that he is Lord of all, then you are saved. Jesus is your Savior and Lord. How can you be sure of this? Because God promised, and God always keeps his promises. Although your relationship with Jesus as the Savior and Lord of your life began at a particular moment in time, you should have an active, growing friendship with him that continues throughout your daily life. This assures you that you will enjoy eternal life in heaven and receive eternal rewards as well.

TODAY'S PLAN

How can you be as sure of your salvation today as when you first believed?

HAND OF GOD

TODAY'S PROMISE

Come and see what our God has done, what awesome miracles he performs for people! —PSALM 66:5

TODAY'S THOUGHT

God works on behalf of his people in miraculous ways. The daily news is filled with all the terrible things that are happening in the world. But if you step back for a moment, you can begin to get a glimpse of God's hand quietly working miracles in many people's lives—including yours—every day. His hand is there, even when you don't see it.

TODAY'S PLAN

Has anything happened in your life recently that might have been the hand of God at work on your behalf?

ETERNITY

TODAY'S PROMISE

This world is not our permanent home; we are looking forward to a home yet to come. —HEBREWS 13:14

TODAY'S THOUGHT

As a heaven-bound follower of Jesus, try to put earth and heaven in perspective. Here, you will probably live for less than a hundred years. In heaven, one hundred *million* years will be just the beginning. If you are going to spend most of your time in heaven, you should spend your time here on earth preparing yourself to live there. Having an eternal perspective will help you live today with the right priorities, for this life is really your preparation for eternity.

TODAY'S PLAN

How can your understanding of eternity change the way you live today?

LOVE

TODAY'S PROMISE

God showed how much he loved us by sending his one and only Son into the world so that we might have eternal life through him. This is real love—not that we loved God, but that he loved us and sent his Son as a sacrifice to take away our sins.

—1 JOHN 4:9-10

TODAY'S THOUGHT

Real love is being willing to sacrifice much— even life itself—for the good of someone else. You know for certain how much God loves you because he allowed his Son to die in your place, to take the punishment for your sin so that you could be free from eternal judgment. Think of it: God sent his Son to die for you so that you could live forever with him. No wonder John wrote, "This is real love"!

TODAY'S PLAN

How can you take some time today to pause and consider God's great love for you?

RESURRECTION

TODAY'S PROMISE

Jesus told her, "I am the resurrection and the life. Anyone who believes in me will live, even after dying."

—JOHN 11:25

TODAY'S THOUGHT

Jesus' resurrection is key to the Christian faith. Just as he promised, Jesus rose from the dead. You can be confident, then, that God will keep all his other promises. And you can be certain of your own resurrection because Jesus has power over death. The resurrection of Jesus proves that he was more than just a human leader; he is the Son of God, and he brings eternal life to all who believe in him.

TODAY'S PLAN

How is Jesus' resurrection the basis of your faith? How does it affect your daily life?

FUTURE

TODAY'S PROMISE

We know that God causes everything to work together for the good of those who love God and are called according to his purpose for them.

—ROMANS 8:28

TODAY'S THOUGHT

When you are absolutely convinced that Jesus died on the cross to spare you from eternal punishment and give you the free gift of eternal life, then the troubles of this world are put into perspective. You know that your future—for all eternity—is secure. This gives you peace no matter what happens in this life, and it changes the way you react to the troubles and trials that come your way.

TODAY'S PLAN

How do God's promises about the future affect the way you live today?

FAITH

TODAY'S PROMISE

Then he said to Thomas, "Put your finger here, and look at my hands. Put your hand into the wound in my side. Don't be faithless any longer. Believe!" "My Lord and my God!" Thomas exclaimed. Then Jesus told him, "You believe because you have seen me. Blessed are those who believe without seeing me." —JOHN 20:27-29

TODAY'S THOUGHT

The strongest faith is based not on physical proof but on spiritual conviction. There is a spiritual element to this world that you cannot see but that is very real. Your faith becomes stronger as the Holy Spirit sharpens your "spiritual vision" so that you can see and experience the results of God working in your own life and in the lives of those around you. God promises to bless those who believe even when their spiritual vision is weak.

TODAY'S PLAN

Is your faith based on seeing or believing?

CONFESSION

TODAY'S PROMISE

If we confess our sins to him, he is faithful and just to forgive us our sins and to cleanse us from all wickedness.

—1 JOHN 1:9

TODAY'S THOUGHT

Confession reveals the sin within your heart. When you acknowledge the ugliness of your sin, it can be embarrassing and sometimes painful. It is never easy to look deep into the dark places of your life, to become vulnerable and open yourself to rebuke. But confession is a necessary part of knowing God, of receiving forgiveness and freedom from sin, of identifying yourself as a follower of Jesus Christ. God's supply of forgiveness far exceeds what your sins demand. No matter how many sins you confess or how often you confess them, God promises to forgive you whenever you ask.

TODAY'S PLAN

What sins do you need to confess to God (or to someone else) today so you can be forgiven?

HEAVEN

TODAY'S PROMISE

There is more than enough room in my Father's home. If this were not so, would I have told you that I am going to prepare a place for you?

—JOHN 14:2

TODAY'S THOUGHT

When you travel, it's comforting to know you have a place to stay at the end of the day. You can have this same comfort for the end of your life's journey. Not only is there a heaven, but Jesus is making preparations there for your arrival. Heaven is not just a paradise you will visit only on vacation. It is an eternal dwelling place where you will live in joyful fellowship with your heavenly Father and your heavenly family. Though death is a great unknown, Jesus Christ has gone before you, and he is preparing a glorious place for you to stay. If you know and love Jesus, you can be confident that your room is ready and waiting.

TODAY'S PLAN

How do you envision the place Jesus is preparing for you in heaven?

EXCUSES

TODAY'S PROMISE

At the name of Jesus every knee should bow, in heaven and on earth and under the earth, and every tongue confess that Jesus Christ is Lord, to the glory of God the Father. —PHILIPPIANS 2:10-11

TODAY'S THOUGHT

People have all kinds of excuses for avoiding Jesus—they're too busy, they see him as the cause of their hardships, they procrastinate, they don't want to give up their favorite vices, or maybe they just don't know where to begin. But the Bible promises that the day will come when you must face Jesus, and he will know whether or not you have declared him Lord of your life. Deal with any excuses you may have today so that you will be ready when that day arrives.

TODAY'S PLAN

Do you make excuses to avoid following Jesus? Will those excuses hold up when you come face-to-face with Jesus?

MERCY

TODAY'S PROMISE

The LORD passed in front of Moses, calling out, "Yahweh! The LORD! The God of compassion and mercy! I am slow to anger and filled with unfailing love and faithfulness." —EXODUS 34:6

TODAY'S THOUGHT

Because of God's love, you are given the free gift of salvation even though you don't deserve it. Because of God's mercy, you are forgiven and freed from guilt. Because of God's kindness, you will be blessed beyond your wildest dreams because he will give you a place in heaven for all eternity.

TODAY'S PLAN

How should God's mercy toward you change the way you live today?

PERFECTION

TODAY'S PROMISE

I don't mean to say that I have already achieved these things or that I have already reached perfection. But I press on to possess that perfection for which Christ Jesus first possessed me. —PHILIPPIANS 3:12

TODAY'S THOUGHT

Many of us strive for perfection in one or more areas of our lives. We want to be the perfect spouse or parent, perform flawlessly on the job, or be supremely skilled at a particular sport or hobby. But here on earth we will always be struggling against the reality of our human-ness and sinful nature, which stand in the way of our quest for perfection. God understands our desire for perfection, and he sent his Son, Jesus, who *is* perfect, holy, and blameless. Through Jesus' death on the cross, God exchanges our human sinfulness for his per-fect holiness.

TODAY'S PLAN

Are you longing for the perfection God promises in heaven?

DEATH

TODAY'S PROMISE

Our dying bodies must be transformed into bodies that will never die; our mortal bodies must be transformed into immortal bodies. Then . . . this Scripture will be fulfilled: "Death is swallowed up in victory. O death, where is your victory? O death, where is your sting?"

—1 CORINTHIANS 15:53-55

TODAY'S THOUGHT

So often we see death as a terrible end, but what an adventure awaits those who love Jesus! When Christians die, they will meet God and live with him forever in heaven. Our bodies will be totally transformed into bodies that will never again be subjected to sin, pain, death, and the limitations of this world.

TODAY'S PLAN

How can you live differently today because of the knowledge that you will live forever with God?

HOLINESS

TODAY'S PROMISE

[God] has reconciled you to himself through the death of Christ in his physical body. As a result, he has brought you into his own presence, and you are holy and blameless as you stand before him without a single fault.
—COLOSSIANS 1:22

TODAY'S THOUGHT

Holiness is much more than the absence of sin; it is the practice of righteousness, purity, and godliness. Holiness is being wholly dedicated and devoted to God, being distinct and separate from the world's way of living, being committed to godly living and purity. When you become a Christian, God makes you holy by forgiving your sins. He looks at you as if you had never sinned. Even though God sees you as holy because of Jesus, you still cannot live a life of perfect holiness. Here on earth, you must strive each day to be more like Jesus.

TODAY'S PLAN

What can you do today to pursue greater holiness?

JESUS

TODAY'S PROMISE

Christ is the visible image of the invisible God. He existed before anything was created and is supreme over all creation. . . . Christ is also the head of the church, which is his body. He is the beginning, supreme over all who rise from the dead. So he is first in everything. For God in all his fullness was pleased to live in Christ, and through him God reconciled everything to himself. He made peace with everything in heaven and on earth by means of Christ's blood on the cross.

—COLOSSIANS 1:15-20

TODAY'S THOUGHT

These verses assure you that everything is under the control of Jesus Christ and everything is possible through him. The more you get to know Jesus, the more you will see how he loves and cares for you and the more confident you will be that he keeps his promises.

TODAY'S PLAN

What are you doing to get to know Jesus better?

DOUBT

TODAY'S PROMISE

When doubts filled my mind, your comfort gave me renewed hope and cheer. —PSALM 94:19

TODAY'S THOUGHT

God doesn't mind when you doubt as long as you continue to seek him in the midst of it. Doubt can become sin if it leads you away from God and into skepticism, cynicism, or hard-heartedness. But doubt can be beneficial if your honest searching leads you to God and a deeper faith.

TODAY'S PLAN

Do you have questions you want to ask God? Go ahead and ask him, and be sure to seek his answers.

HEAVEN

TODAY'S PROMISE

I heard a loud shout from the throne, saying, "Look, God's home is now among his people! He will live with them, and they will be his people. God himself will be with them. He will wipe every tear from their eyes, and there will be no more death or sorrow or crying or pain. All these things are gone forever." —REVELATION 21:3-4

TODAY'S THOUGHT

Scripture promises that one day God will remove all the sin and struggle from this fallen world and create a new heaven and a new earth. God will actually live among his people. The best this world has to offer can't even begin to compare with the glory that is to come!

TODAY'S PLAN

Can you imagine what a perfect life in a perfect world would be like?

APPROVAL

TODAY'S PROMISE

The master said, "Well done, my good and faithful servant. You have been faithful in handling this small amount, so now I will give you many more responsibilities. Let's celebrate together!"

—MATTHEW 25:23

TODAY'S THOUGHT

Those who consistently do a good job can usually be trusted with more freedom and responsibility. Their work receives approval from someone who supervises or oversees them. In the same way, the more you serve God, the more he will reward your faithfulness and give you opportunities to serve him with greater freedom and responsibility. Remember that God's love for you never changes, but his approval of your work is based on how well you serve him.

TODAY'S PLAN

How can you better serve God today to gain his approval?

CHARACTER

TODAY'S PROMISE

Don't make judgments about anyone ahead of time—before the Lord returns. For he will bring our darkest secrets to light and will reveal our private motives. Then God will give to each one whatever praise is due.
—1 CORINTHIANS 4:5

TODAY'S THOUGHT

Character is who you actually are—the sum total of everything that distinguishes you from everyone else. Your reputation—what other people say about you—is often a good indication of your character. But character is also who you desire to become. If you strive for good character—or better yet, godly character—you are working toward moral excellence. You work hard all your life for excellence in many areas, so it only makes sense to work hard at moral excellence. You want to be known as someone who has integrity, kindness, love, faithfulness—the character qualities that really matter.

TODAY'S PLAN

How do you think others would describe your character?

HOPE

TODAY'S PROMISE

Through Christ you have come to trust in God. And you have placed your faith and hope in God because he raised Christ from the dead and gave him great glory.

—1 PETER 1:21

TODAY'S THOUGHT

For a prisoner on death row, a pardon offers the hope of freedom. We were once spiritual prisoners facing eternal death because of our sin, but God gave us ultimate hope by forgiving our sins so we can be with him forever in heaven. When life seems impossible, God gives eternal hope. Hope is essential for persevering through the tough times. Without hope, we would give up. Hope simply requires that we trust in the only One who is able to grant it.

TODAY'S PLAN

Is the hope that you have today strong enough to get you through any tough times ahead?

PERSECUTION

TODAY'S PROMISE

God blesses you when people mock you and persecute you and lie about you and say all sorts of evil things against you because you are my followers.

—MATTHEW 5:11

TODAY'S THOUGHT

If you are being persecuted for your faith, be encouraged by the fact that many other faithful believers are also standing strong in the face of persecution. The Bible says that suffering persecution for Jesus' sake is an honor. It is evidence of the depth of your love and commitment to Jesus, so it is actually a privilege to suffer for him. Persecution also helps you remember and be grateful for the depth of suffering Jesus went through for you.

TODAY'S PLAN

If you suffer persecution because of your faith, do you see it as an honor?

JOY

TODAY'S PROMISE

I will be filled with joy because of you. I will sing praises to your name, O Most High. —PSALM 9:2

TODAY'S THOUGHT

Some aspects of the Christian life we view with appropriate seriousness—sin and its consequences, church discipline, fighting against evil. But the Christian life also holds great delights—the knowledge that the God of the universe loves you, has a plan for you, and has made this wonderful world for you to live in. In fact, God wants you to serve him enthusiastically, joyfully, and with great delight. God promises to fill you with the joy he delights to see in his followers.

TODAY'S PLAN

What aspects of your faith give you joy? What can you do today to make sure that those around you see your joy?

MEDITATION

TODAY'S PROMISE

I wait quietly before God, for my victory comes from him. . . . Let all that I am wait quietly before God, for my hope is in him.
—PSALM 62:1, 5

TODAY'S THOUGHT

Meditation is setting aside time to intentionally think about God, talk to him, and listen to him. When you make time to meditate on God, you distance yourself from the distractions and noise of the world and move within range of his voice. You prepare your mind to be taught and your desires to be molded into what God desires. As a result, God promises to change you, and your thoughts and actions will fall in line with his will. Meditation is more than just the study of God. It is intimate communion with him, which ultimately leads to godly living.

TODAY'S PLAN

How can you make it a daily habit to meditate on God?

IMPOSSIBILITY

TODAY'S PROMISE

Nothing is impossible with God.   —LUKE 1:37

TODAY'S THOUGHT

Are you facing a problem or situation that seems
   impossible? Trust that God can do the impossible
   and that he wants to work in your life. But if he
   chooses not to take away this particular obstacle,
   trust that he knows what is best for you. While
   impossible situations seem to limit you and
   exhaust your resources, they set the stage for
   God to do what is humanly unimaginable—such
   as using his supernatural power to work miracles,
   demonstrate his love, give salvation, meet needs,
   and change lives.

TODAY'S PLAN

*What seems impossible in your life today? Have you
   asked God to work the impossible in you?*

COMMUNITY

TODAY'S PROMISE

You must call a meeting of the church. I will be present with you in spirit, and so will the power of our Lord Jesus.
— 1 CORINTHIANS 5:4

TODAY'S THOUGHT

We were created for community. Jesus commissioned the church to be a body of believers, not a collection of individuals. Being connected to other people in loving relationships is important to living a life of hope. Living in isolation makes us vulnerable to discouragement and despair. When we are connected to a community of believers, we are able to worship together, to support one another, and to experience fellowship that keep us strong in the faith even during the most difficult times. Because Jesus promises to be with us when we gather as a body of believers, it is in community that we can experience God's presence in a unique and powerful way.

TODAY'S PLAN

Are you regularly experiencing God's presence within a Christian community?

SALVATION

TODAY'S PROMISE

If you confess with your mouth that Jesus is Lord and believe in your heart that God raised him from the dead, you will be saved. For it is by believing in your heart that you are made right with God, and it is by confessing with your mouth that you are saved.
—ROMANS 10:9-10

TODAY'S THOUGHT

There is only one way to be certain that you will go to heaven instead of hell when you die. You must believe in your heart that Jesus died and rose again to save you from the consequences of your sin, and you must be willing to confess your sin to him as well as confess your faith to others. By taking these steps in faith, you secure your salvation and your place in eternity with God.

TODAY'S PLAN

Have you confessed Jesus Christ as your Lord and Savior?

ETERNITY

TODAY'S PROMISE

Anyone who does what pleases God will live forever.

—1 JOHN 2:17

TODAY'S THOUGHT

When you obey God, you are able to enjoy life the way he meant it to be enjoyed. Your relationships are more fulfilling, your life is full of integrity, and your conscience is clear. More important, you will be able to enjoy life with God in a perfect world for all eternity.

TODAY'S PLAN

How often do you obey God because of his promises for eternity?

MAY

GRACE

TODAY'S PROMISE

God saved you by his grace when you believed. And you can't take credit for this; it is a gift from God.

—EPHESIANS 2:8

TODAY'S THOUGHT

Remember that God saves you because of his grace alone. God approves of you not because of what you do or don't do, but because he loves you and has forgiven all your sins. The fact that this is God's gift and not the product of your own effort gives you great comfort, security, and hope. When you accept God's grace just as you accept any other gift, you will fully enjoy its benefits.

TODAY'S PLAN

How can you pass along the gift of God's grace to someone else today?

HOLY SPIRIT

TODAY'S PROMISE

Each of you must repent of your sins, turn to God, and be baptized in the name of Jesus Christ to show that you have received forgiveness for your sins. Then you will receive the gift of the Holy Spirit. This promise is to you, and to your children, and even to the Gentiles—all who have been called by the Lord our God.
—ACTS 2:38-39

TODAY'S THOUGHT

When Jesus ascended into heaven, his physical presence left the earth. But he promised to send the Holy Spirit so that his presence would still be among humankind and would literally live within believers. When you believe this is true and place your trust in God, he sends his Holy Spirit to live in you. The Spirit assures you of God's constant presence and help in your life.

TODAY'S PLAN

Have you turned to God, received forgiveness, and believed in Jesus? Then you have the Holy Spirit living in you.

DELIVERANCE

TODAY'S PROMISE

The angel of the LORD is a guard; he surrounds and defends all who fear him. —PSALM 34:7

TODAY'S THOUGHT

The God who has already defeated evil is always with you. Because you have his presence in your life, you can be sure he will deliver you from evil. Sometimes God will step into a situation to rescue you. Sometimes he will send supernatural help through angels, his warriors who are in constant battle against Satan and the powers of evil. No matter how God chooses to work, he is always with you and promises to deliver you.

TODAY'S PLAN

How can you make a daily habit of seeing God's hand of deliverance working on your behalf through the events in your life?

NEIGHBORS

TODAY'S PROMISE

Love your neighbor as yourself. —MATTHEW 22:39

TODAY'S THOUGHT

Jesus said that loving your neighbor as yourself is the second greatest commandment, after loving God wholeheartedly. God knows that your first instinct is to take care of yourself. If you can learn to meet the needs of others in the same way you meet your own needs, then you will be fulfilling Jesus' command. If you love others the way God intended, you will also be carrying out God's other instructions. Love directed inward goes nowhere, but love directed outward changes the world one person at a time.

TODAY'S PLAN

How can you show greater love to those around you?

FEAR OF GOD

TODAY'S PROMISE

How joyful are those who fear the LORD—all who follow his ways!
—PSALM 128:1

TODAY'S THOUGHT

Does it seem ironic that those who "fear" the Lord actually experience more joy? Fearing God, however, is not the same as being afraid of him. If you are afraid of God, you will stay away from him. Fearing God means being awed by his power, mercy, and goodness. This draws you closer to him, within the circle of blessings he gives to all who love him. Fear of God is like the respect you have for a beloved teacher, coach, parent, or mentor. Your respect motivates you both to do your best and to avoid doing something that would offend or hurt that person. You fear God because of his awesome power, and you love God for the way he blesses you.

TODAY'S PLAN

How can you increase your fear of God and experience more joy as a result?

BLESSINGS

TODAY'S PROMISE

May God our Father and the Lord Jesus Christ give you grace and peace. . . . When you believed in Christ, he identified you as his own by giving you the Holy Spirit, whom he promised long ago. The Spirit is God's guarantee that he will give us the inheritance he promised and that he has purchased us to be his own people. —EPHESIANS 1:2, 13-14

TODAY'S THOUGHT

God's love is like a vast ocean. He sends wave after wave of blessings to flow over you. Just as the movement of the ocean is constant, God's blessings are constant, even when you are not aware of them. Scripture is full of the blessings God promises to those who love him, including his presence, his grace, and his peace. He also promises you his Holy Spirit, who opens your eyes to the blessings that surround you every day.

TODAY'S PLAN

Make a list of God's blessings to you. How many can you name?

OPPORTUNITIES

TODAY'S PROMISE

Pharaoh said to Joseph, "Since God has revealed the meaning of the dreams to you, clearly no one else is as intelligent or wise as you are. You will be in charge of my court, and all my people will take orders from you. Only I, sitting on my throne, will have a rank higher than yours."

—GENESIS 41:39-40

TODAY'S THOUGHT

Responsibility is one of the keys to opening doors of opportunity. Joseph was unjustly thrown into prison. He could have become bitter and done nothing. Instead, at every opportunity he earned others' trust because of his responsibility, and eventually rose to great prominence in Egypt. When you handle even your minor, day-to-day responsibilities well, you can expect much greater opportunities.

TODAY'S PLAN

How responsible are you in handling every opportunity, both big and small?

HOLY SPIRIT

TODAY'S PROMISE

When the Father sends the Advocate as my representative—that is, the Holy Spirit—he will teach you everything and will remind you of everything I have told you.

—JOHN 14:26

TODAY'S THOUGHT

God promised the gift of the Holy Spirit to his people, but the gift was not given until after Jesus rose from the dead and ascended into heaven. Anyone who believes in Jesus Christ as Savior also has the Holy Spirit living inside them. The Holy Spirit helps you understand the deep truths of God, convicts you of sin, teaches you how to live a life that pleases God, helps you pray, enables you to resist temptation, and assures you that you are a child of God.

Thank God for giving you his Holy Spirit, and pray expectantly that he will release more and more of the Spirit's power in your life.

TODAY'S PLAN

How can you tap into more of the Holy Spirit's power?

RECONCILIATION

TODAY'S PROMISE

God has given us this task of reconciling people to him. For God was in Christ, reconciling the world to himself, no longer counting people's sins against them. . . . We speak for Christ when we plead, "Come back to God!" For God made Christ, who never sinned, to be the offering for our sin, so that we could be made right with God through Christ.
—2 CORINTHIANS 5:18-21

TODAY'S THOUGHT

Reconciliation between two people divided by conflict is possible only when one of them makes the first move—a hand extended, a phone call, words of forgiveness. Sin separates you from God. The relationship is broken, and someone has to make the first move. You are the one who needed to be reconciled, but God made the first move, sending his Son, Jesus Christ, to bridge the divide between himself and you.

TODAY'S PLAN

God has made the first move toward reconciliation with you. Have you made the next move?

HAPPINESS

TODAY'S PROMISE

I know the LORD is always with me. . . . He is right beside me. No wonder my heart is glad, and I rejoice.

—PSALM 16:8-9

TODAY'S THOUGHT

Is happiness merely a passing emotion, or is it a permanent state of being? The Bible says it can be both. There is happiness that is a reaction to happenings, which is temporary and volatile; and there is happiness that is above and beyond happenings, which is strong and lasting. If happiness based on happenings is all we have, we must keep finding good things and good experiences to keep us happy. Those who know the joy that comes from God don't need experiences to keep them happy. They have inner joy because they know that no matter what happens, God is with them and promises lasting hope and happiness.

TODAY'S PLAN

Are you looking in the right place for lasting happiness?

ENDURANCE

TODAY'S PROMISE

Patient endurance is what you need now, so that you will continue to do God's will. Then you will receive all that he has promised. —HEBREWS 10:36

TODAY'S THOUGHT

Endurance is an essential quality of Jesus' followers. Though you have the promise of eternal life, you also live here and now in a fallen world where the powers of sin and Satan are out to destroy your faith. God promises that if you endure in your faith, not only will you survive but you will reign with Christ forever!

TODAY'S PLAN

What can you do today to increase your spiritual endurance?

MOTIVES

TODAY'S PROMISE

The LORD's light penetrates the human spirit, exposing every hidden motive. —PROVERBS 20:27

TODAY'S THOUGHT

When someone gives a thousand dollars to a charity, it seems like such a good and selfless act. But one person may do it in order to earn a tax break; another may do it to win political favor; another person may in fact do it out of deep compassion for the poor. The same act can be set in motion by very different motives. The Bible teaches that God is as interested in our motives as he is in our behavior. Selfish and sinful motives eventually produce selfish and sinful behavior, but good and godly motives result in true good works.

TODAY'S PLAN

Evaluate every decision you make today. How many of your actions are based on good motives rather than selfish ones?

POWER OF GOD

TODAY'S PROMISE

With God's help we will do mighty things.

—PSALM 60:12

TODAY'S THOUGHT

Try not to look at the size of your problem but at the size of your God. When there are so many seemingly impossible things to be done, remember that you have a powerful God who will help you accomplish them.

TODAY'S PLAN

How can you rely on God's power today?

CHALLENGES

TODAY'S PROMISE

In your strength I can crush an army; with my God I can scale any wall. —2 SAMUEL 22:30

TODAY'S THOUGHT

Every day brings some kind of challenge. You may not rule a nation or run a large corporation, but you do face tough situations, difficult people, or subtle temptations. Challenges keep you from getting too comfortable or too accepting of the status quo; they force you into uncharted waters. Without God's leading, this would be frightening, but with God it can be a great adventure. So whatever challenge you are facing, make sure you head into it with God at your side.

TODAY'S PLAN

What challenge, big or small, are you facing today? Try to picture God by your side, and then move forward with confidence.

PROTECTION

TODAY'S PROMISE

My help comes from the LORD, who made heaven and earth! He will not let you stumble; the one who watches over you will not slumber. Indeed, he who watches over Israel never slumbers or sleeps. The LORD himself watches over you! The LORD stands beside you as your protective shade. . . . The LORD keeps watch over you as you come and go, both now and forever. —PSALM 121:2-5, 8

TODAY'S THOUGHT

God promises to protect and keep safe those who love him. But the ultimate fulfillment of this promise comes as God safeguards your soul so that your body and soul will live forever with him in heaven. No matter what might happen to your earthly body, you must commit your-self to obeying God to ensure that your soul will be in the right place for eternity.

TODAY'S PLAN

Are you more concerned about the safety and protec-tion of your body or your soul? Make it your greatest goal to get both body and soul safely into heaven.

SUCCESS

TODAY'S PROMISE

Now all glory to God, who is able to keep you from falling away and will bring you with great joy into his glorious presence without a single fault. —JUDE 1:24

TODAY'S THOUGHT

The world defines success as an abundance of achievements and possessions, and it defines failure as a lack of achievements and possessions. God defines success as obedience to him, which results in love, godly character, righteous living, salvation, and eternal life in heaven. God defines failure as rejecting him. When you live according to God's definition of success, your failures will be only temporary.

TODAY'S PLAN

What one thing can you do today to focus on God's definition of success?

SELF-CONTROL

TODAY'S PROMISE

Let the Holy Spirit guide your lives. Then you won't be doing what your sinful nature craves. . . . Those who belong to Christ Jesus have nailed the passions and desires of their sinful nature to his cross and crucified them there. —GALATIANS 5:16, 24

TODAY'S THOUGHT

Because you were born with a sinful nature, you will always struggle to do what is right instead of what is wrong. God understands your weaknesses, and he promises to give you his Holy Spirit to help you develop the desire to please him. As the Spirit leads you to obey God, you will develop more self-control and greater strength to fight and win the battle with your sinful nature.

TODAY'S PLAN

In what area of your life do you need to ask the Holy Spirit to help you gain more self-control?

COMPASSION

TODAY'S PROMISE

Moved with compassion, Jesus reached out and touched him. "I am willing," he said. "Be healed!"

—MARK 1:41

TODAY'S THOUGHT

Compassion is deeply seated in your emotions. It is when your heart is truly touched and you feel true caring for someone in need. Compassion can be a litmus test of your commitment and desire to love others as Christ loves you. To be Christlike is to show the same compassion that Jesus showed toward the poor, the sick, the needy—those who cannot help themselves. If you are not moved by the incredible needs and hurts of the people around you, you might develop a heart of stone that could become too hard to respond either to God or to others. Let Christ's compassion keep your heart soft and responsive.

TODAY'S PLAN

Is your heart becoming more compassionate toward those in need?

ENEMIES

TODAY'S PROMISE

Don't repay evil for evil. Don't retaliate with insults when people insult you. Instead, pay them back with a blessing. That is what God has called you to do, and he will bless you for it. —1 PETER 3:9

TODAY'S THOUGHT

Showing love to your enemies seems completely unreasonable—unless you realize that you were once an enemy of God until he forgave you. When you love your enemy, you see that person as Christ does—someone in need of grace and forgiveness. Getting to that point takes prayer. When you pray for someone, you can't help but feel compassion for them. When you respond with prayer and blessing instead of retaliation when someone hurts you, God promises to bless you. God can even turn your enemy into your friend.

TODAY'S PLAN

How can you show God's grace to someone you consider an enemy?

SALVATION

TODAY'S PROMISE

Everyone has sinned; we all fall short of God's glorious standard. . . . If you confess with your mouth that Jesus is Lord and believe in your heart that God raised him from the dead, you will be saved.

—ROMANS 3:23; 10:9

TODAY'S THOUGHT

Understanding the difference between God's unconditional love for all people and his salvation of only those who confess and believe is a matter of life and death. God loves you unconditionally, but he does not approve of your sinful behavior. You must understand that your sin separates you from God and that Jesus died and rose again to take away your sin and restore you to him. Then you will realize how much God values you. When you confess your sins to him, seek his forgiveness, and commit to following Jesus, you will receive salvation and eternal life in heaven.

TODAY'S PLAN

Have you experienced both God's love and his salvation?

ACCEPTANCE

TODAY'S PROMISE

Those the Father has given me will come to me, and I will never reject them. —JOHN 6:37

TODAY'S THOUGHT

God accepts everyone who comes to him in faith, even those who previously rejected him. You can approach God knowing that he will gladly welcome you and will always accept you. God will never say, "Sorry, I don't have time for you" or "Don't bother me." He always listens, always responds, always loves, always is there for you. God does not turn away but rather embraces you so you can receive all the blessings he promises you. In his open arms, you also find the ultimate example of how to accept others.

TODAY'S PLAN

Do you struggle to believe that God promises to accept you, no matter what? Run to his open arms today, and feel his acceptance.

GIVING

TODAY'S PROMISE

Give, and you will receive. Your gift will return to you in full—pressed down, shaken together to make room for more, running over, and poured into your lap. The amount you give will determine the amount you get back.

—LUKE 6:38

TODAY'S THOUGHT

The act of giving creates a cycle of blessing. As God has given abundantly to you, so you give abundantly back to him as well as to others. This in turn leads those people to give abundantly to God and to other people. God promises that as you give, you will also receive blessing in return.

TODAY'S PLAN

What can you do today to start a cycle of abundant giving?

DISCERNMENT

TODAY'S PROMISE

Let those who are wise understand these things. Let those with discernment listen carefully. The paths of the LORD are true and right, and righteous people live by walking in them. But in those paths sinners stumble and fall.
—HOSEA 14:9

TODAY'S THOUGHT

Discernment is the ability to distinguish between right and wrong by training and disciplining your conscience, mind, senses, and body. The Bible says that discernment is necessary for you to mature in your faith. When you develop discernment, you are able to recognize temptation before it has engulfed you. You learn to recognize the difference between truth and lies, between God's voice and the voices of sin and Satan. When you practice discernment, you avoid the pitfalls and confusion that so many people fall into. You walk in God's ways, which are true and right and lead you to a better life.

TODAY'S PLAN

How can you practice discernment today?

PATIENCE

TODAY'S PROMISE

Patient endurance is what you need now, so that you will continue to do God's will. Then you will receive all that he has promised. —HEBREWS 10:36

TODAY'S THOUGHT

Patience is evidence of strong character. You cannot have endurance or perseverance without first developing patience. As a Christian, your faith will be tested time after time. But as you pass each test, you will develop more patience, which will build greater strength and perseverance for when you are tested again. When you are patient, you will eventually receive the fulfillment of all of God's promises to you.

TODAY'S PLAN

In what area of your life do you need to practice patience today?

JUSTICE

TODAY'S PROMISE

The LORD loves justice, and he will never abandon the godly. He will keep them safe forever, but the children of the wicked will die. —PSALM 37:28

TODAY'S THOUGHT

God judges all injustice as sin. As a just and holy God, he cannot allow injustice or sin to go unpunished. He promises to punish all those who are unjust. Some may begin to experience their punishment on earth, but all unjust people will receive their full punishment in eternity. If you are struggling with an injustice done to you or someone you love, be assured that one day God will set everything right and will vindicate the godly.

TODAY'S PLAN

Is there a situation in your life in which you are longing for God's justice?

FAITH

TODAY'S PROMISE

If you look carefully into the perfect law that sets you free, and if you do what it says and don't forget what you heard, then God will bless you for doing it.

—JAMES 1:25

TODAY'S THOUGHT

Faith is like a muscle; it gets stronger the more you exercise it. When you do what God asks you to do and see him bless you as a result of your obedience, your faith grows stronger. The next time God asks you to do something, you will have more confidence to take that leap of faith.

TODAY'S PLAN

How can you exercise your faith this week?

CHANGE

TODAY'S PROMISE

Whatever is good and perfect comes down to us from God our Father, who created all the lights in the heavens. He never changes or casts a shifting shadow. —JAMES 1:17

TODAY'S THOUGHT

The character of God never changes, thus it is completely reliable. What great comfort! No matter how your life changes, no matter what new situation you face, God is with you. You can always count on his unchanging promises to help, guide, and take care of you.

TODAY'S PLAN

How can you take comfort in God's unchanging character in your life today?

COURAGE

TODAY'S PROMISE

Be strong and courageous! Do not be afraid or discouraged. For the LORD your God is with you wherever you go.
—JOSHUA 1:9

TODAY'S THOUGHT

Throughout your life, you will find yourself in scary situations—mortal danger, extreme stress, major illness, financial troubles, or any number of problems. True courage comes from understanding that God is stronger than your biggest problem or fiercest enemy, and he uses his power to help you. Instead of misplaced confidence in your own strength, courage is well-placed confidence in God's strength. While fear comes from feeling alone against a great threat, courage comes from knowing that God is beside you, helping you fight the threat. To have more courage, focus more on God's presence and less on the problem.

TODAY'S PLAN

What scary situation are you facing today? Where can you get the courage to overcome it?

JOY

TODAY'S PROMISE

The LORD your God will delight in you if you obey his voice and keep the commands and decrees written in this Book of Instruction, and if you turn to the LORD your God with all your heart and soul.

—DEUTERONOMY 30:10

TODAY'S THOUGHT

Can finite, sinful human beings truly bring joy and delight to the Lord, the Creator of the universe? God says yes. He created you because he wants to have a relationship with you, to delight in being with you. But a good relationship works in both directions. A relationship that brings joy to God is built on trust, regular communication, honesty, humility, service, and unconditional love.

TODAY'S PLAN

Do you think you are bringing God joy?

HURT

TODAY'S PROMISE

So we don't look at the troubles we can see now; rather, we fix our gaze on things that cannot be seen. For the things we see now will soon be gone, but the things we cannot see will last forever.

—2 CORINTHIANS 4:18

TODAY'S THOUGHT

God promises that the troubles looming in front of you today won't last forever. Your goal, then, is to turn your focus away from your hurt and look instead to those things that will last forever—God's love, his gift of salvation, his care for you, and eternity in heaven with him. When you live with this perspective, you see your hurts and troubles as part of this temporary world and you know they won't last. Then you can have greater hope and confidence in God's promise of a world where there will be no more hurt or pain.

TODAY'S PLAN

How can you focus on God today instead of on your hurt?

PROTECTION

TODAY'S PROMISE

*Don't be afraid of those who want to kill your body;
they cannot touch your soul. Fear only God, who
can destroy both soul and body in hell. . . . Not a
single sparrow can fall to the ground without your
Father knowing it. And the very hairs on your
head are all numbered. So don't be afraid; you
are more valuable to God than a whole flock of
sparrows.* —MATTHEW 10:28-31

TODAY'S THOUGHT

Although God often protects you from physical harm, he is more concerned about protecting
your soul from eternal harm. When you commit
to following his ways, he commits to bringing you safely into eternity with him. So ask
God for his protection. He is strong where
you are weak. He is your safe haven when you
are vulnerable and under attack. You have the
power and presence of God protecting you.

TODAY'S PLAN

*In what ways has God protected you in the past, from
both physical and spiritual harm?*

JUNE

REPENTANCE

TODAY'S PROMISE

Now repent of your sins and turn to God, so that your sins may be wiped away. —ACTS 3:19

TODAY'S THOUGHT

One of the first steps in repentance is confession. You must be humbly honest with God and sincerely sorry for your sins—both the ones you know about and the ones you are unaware you have committed. Genuine repentance also requires a heart that truly longs for change. Repentance brings forgiveness and restores your relationship with God, which renews your strength and spirit. When you repent, God removes your guilt, heals your broken soul, and restores your joy.

TODAY'S PLAN

Are you truly sorry for your sins? Have you repented and asked God to forgive you?

EVIL

TODAY'S PROMISE

[Put] on the belt of truth and the body armor of God's righteousness. For shoes, put on the peace that comes from the Good News. . . . Hold up the shield of faith. . . . Put on salvation as your helmet, and take the sword of the Spirit, which is the word of God. Pray in the Spirit at all times.

—EPHESIANS 6:14-18

TODAY'S THOUGHT

Here the Bible gives us a comprehensive list of resources that God promises to believers. Spiritual forces of evil lurk behind many of the conflicts you face. You should respond by fighting the evil itself. When God's resources are mobilized, evil can be held in check.

TODAY'S PLAN

Do you have a battle plan in place to combat the evil forces around you?

GUIDANCE

Trust in the LORD with all your heart; do not depend on your own understanding. Seek his will in all you do, and he will show you which path to take.

—PROVERBS 3:5-6

TODAY'S THOUGHT

In order to get good guidance, you have to know where to put your trust. Someone who is traveling in unfamiliar territory must rely on accurate maps and signs to arrive at the destination. Someone who is critically ill must rely on a medical expert to prescribe the proper treatment. In the same way, you must realize your own spiritual limitations and rely on God's Word—the believer's instruction manual—in matters of faith. You can't understand all the complexities of life, but the Lord does. Trust him to guide you and show you the best way to go.

TODAY'S PLAN

How can you rely today on the expertise of God's guidance?

ATTITUDE

TODAY'S PROMISE

So, my dear brothers and sisters, be strong and immovable. Always work enthusiastically for the Lord, for you know that nothing you do for the Lord is ever useless.
—1 CORINTHIANS 15:58

TODAY'S THOUGHT

Attitude is important because it affects your thoughts, motives, and actions. As a believer, you can maintain a positive attitude that is based on the fact that the God of the universe created you, loves you, and promises you salvation and eternal life. God is working for you, not against you. Remind yourself of these truths every day. It will positively affect your attitude, which will positively affect the way you live and serve God.

TODAY'S PLAN

On a scale of one to ten, how is your attitude? How can you bring it up a few notches today?

CARE

TODAY'S PROMISE

I will be your God throughout your lifetime—until your hair is white with age. I made you, and I will care for you. —ISAIAH 46:4

TODAY'S THOUGHT

The God who made you shows his care for you by protecting, providing, and preserving. You can share God's care with others by doing the same for them. You can protect by being kind, helpful, and willing to reach out. You can provide by giving of your time, treasure, and talents to those in need. You can preserve by helping to maintain harmony through your words and actions.

TODAY'S PLAN

List the ways God cares for you. How can you care for others in the same way?

GRIEF

TODAY'S PROMISE

God blesses those who mourn, for they will be comforted.

—MATTHEW 5:4

TODAY'S THOUGHT

Grief brings suffering, anxiety, confusion, rest-
lessness, pain, heartache, and usually plenty
of tears. Some grief, like that of losing a loved
one, can be understood only by those who have
walked its dark valley before you. Grief is like
a stabbing pain. It tortures your soul and robs
you of the joy of living. But you can find this
theme throughout the Bible: Even when you
go through dark times of grief, God is with you,
blessing you with comfort and hope.

TODAY'S PLAN

How can you look for God's blessing in the midst of grief?

OBEDIENCE

TODAY'S PROMISE

When you obey my commandments, you remain in my love. . . . I have told you these things so that you will be filled with my joy. Yes, your joy will overflow!

—JOHN 15:10-11

TODAY'S THOUGHT

Obedience expresses your love for God. But obeying God should not be confused with earning his love through good works. You obey God because he already loves you, not because it will make him love you. As you obey, God promises to give you the joy that comes from living in relationship with him.

TODAY'S PLAN

How can you make obedience to God a priority today?

CREATIVITY

TODAY'S PROMISE

We are God's masterpiece. He has created us anew in Christ Jesus, so we can do the good things he planned for us long ago. —EPHESIANS 2:10

TODAY'S THOUGHT

Creativity is built into every human being. God created you, so you are a product of his creativity! God wants you to use the unique gifts he fashioned in you to help and serve others. God gives you the gift of creativity so that you can express yourself in potentially millions of different ways—through worship, singing, loving, helping, playing music, crafting things, thinking through problems. You should express your creativity in God-honoring ways because it is an extension of a characteristic of God. As God's creation, you have a responsibility to reflect God's creative nature in appropriate ways.

TODAY'S PLAN

In what areas are you creative? How can you use your creativity to help others?

MIRACLES

TODAY'S PROMISE

I will praise you, LORD, with all my heart; I will tell of all the marvelous things you have done.

—PSALM 9:1

TODAY'S THOUGHT

When you ask God for a miracle, you can't know whether or not God in his infinite wisdom will choose to perform that miracle. But you can know that God's love for you is eternal and unchanging. You can therefore trust that God is doing good things in your life even when he doesn't give you exactly what you pray for. The greatest miracle of all is the miracle of God's love for sinners, and that is one you can experience every day.

TODAY'S PLAN

Are you noticing and enjoying the daily miracle of God's love?

JUNE 10

QUITTING

TODAY'S PROMISE

Since Christ suffered physical pain, you must arm yourselves with the same attitude he had, and be ready to suffer, too. For if you have suffered physically for Christ, you have finished with sin. —1 PETER 4:1

TODAY'S THOUGHT

When God has called you to a task, you should not give up. You would not only miss the great blessings of reaching your goal, but you might also incur discipline for not trusting God to help you get there. Just because God asks you to do something doesn't mean it will be easy. Often, the more important the task, the harder it is. If you know God is calling you to a certain task or taking you in a new direction, don't give up just because the going gets tough. Your suffering tells you that you are headed in the right direction. Keep moving forward in faith.

TODAY'S PLAN

How can you know when to quit and when to keep going?

LIMITATIONS

TODAY'S PROMISE

Each one of you will put to flight a thousand of the enemy, for the LORD your God fights for you, just as he has promised.
— JOSHUA 23:10

TODAY'S THOUGHT

You can take courage from the fact that God fights for you, regardless of the odds against you. The Bible gives us many examples: God used the young boy David to overcome the giant Goliath; God used Gideon's three hundred soldiers to defeat the countless thousands of Midianite soldiers; and God used the twelve disciples to establish the whole church. You don't have to be above average for God to do great things through you. Knowing that God works through you despite your limitations is a great encouragement.

TODAY'S PLAN

What limitations seem to be holding you back today?

SALVATION

TODAY'S PROMISE

Everyone who calls on the name of the LORD will be saved. —ROMANS 10:13

TODAY'S THOUGHT

It seems too easy. The greatest gift God could ever offer—life in a perfect world—is absolutely free. God's Word promises salvation—the guarantee of a perfect life in heaven for eternity—to everyone who asks Jesus to forgive their sins. Call out to him in prayer, and tell him that you want him to save you. He promises that he will.

TODAY'S PLAN

Have you accepted God's greatest gift?

ANGER

TODAY'S PROMISE

*The LORD passed in front of Moses, calling out,
"Yahweh! The LORD! The God of compassion
and mercy! I am slow to anger and filled with
unfailing love and faithfulness. I lavish unfailing
love to a thousand generations. I forgive iniquity,
rebellion, and sin. But I do not excuse the
guilty."* —EXODUS 34:6-7

TODAY'S THOUGHT

Because God is perfectly holy, he cannot tolerate sin. Therefore, any kind of sin angers him.
But he is ready to forgive sin because he is also
kind and merciful. Those who humbly confess
their sins and turn to God in faith receive
his abundant love and mercy instead of his
anger.

TODAY'S PLAN

*Do you have sins that need to be forgiven? Ask God today
for his mercy and forgiveness.*

REMEMBERING

TODAY'S PROMISE

Remember the things I have done in the past. For I alone am God! I am God, and there is none like me.

—ISAIAH 46:9

TODAY'S THOUGHT

It is easy to forget about things that aren't important to you, so make sure that God is the most important thing in your life. Then you will be more likely to remember how he has worked in your life before and to go to him first when you need help now. You can keep your focus on God by remembering how you have seen his hand at work in your past, by telling others what he is doing in your life now, by meditating on his word to see how he has worked throughout history, and by sharing his blessings with future generations. When you do these things, you help yourself and others acknowledge God's hand in the past, the present, and the future.

TODAY'S PLAN

When was the last time you really took notice of God's hand at work in your life?

CIRCUMSTANCES

TODAY'S PROMISE

Even though the fig trees have no blossoms, and there are no grapes on the vines; even though the olive crop fails, and the fields lie empty and barren; even though the flocks die in the fields, and the cattle barns are empty, yet I will rejoice in the LORD! I will be joyful in the God of my salvation! The Sovereign LORD is my strength!

—HABAKKUK 3:17-19

TODAY'S THOUGHT

The more you despair in hard times, the more they drag you down. The more you reach out to God with hope and gratitude that your circumstances are temporary, the more your perspective and attitude will change. No matter what your current circumstances, you can respond joyfully to the God who offers you peace of heart and mind.

TODAY'S PLAN

How can you focus more on the blessings of your relationship with God and less on the frustrations of your circumstances?

SACRIFICE

TODAY'S PROMISE

Just as each person is destined to die once and after that comes judgment, so also Christ died once for all time as a sacrifice to take away the sins of many people. He will come again, not to deal with our sins, but to bring salvation to all who are eagerly waiting for him.

—HEBREWS 9:27-28

TODAY'S THOUGHT

In the Old Testament, God's people offered sacrifices to him as part of their worship. The blood of an animal was shed as a substitute for the punishment the people deserved for their sin. All the sacrifices of the Old Testament anticipated the ultimate sacrifice of God's own Son, Jesus, on the cross for the sins of the world. Whenever you must sacrifice or give up something, you can be reminded in some small way of God's greatest sacrifice and his promise of eternal life in heaven because of it.

TODAY'S PLAN

What can you sacrifice today to remind you of God's greatest sacrifice?

FELLOWSHIP

TODAY'S PROMISE

If we are living in the light, as God is in the light, then we have fellowship with each other, and the blood of Jesus, his Son, cleanses us from all sin.

—1 JOHN 1:7

TODAY'S THOUGHT

God created you for relationship. You cannot mature in your faith by yourself, without the help and influence of other Christians. Fellowship with other believers is necessary to keep you accountable, to help you learn God's Word correctly, to pray for each other's needs, to encourage one another, and to help you grow as a Christian.

TODAY'S PLAN

Do you spend enough time in fellowship with other believers to keep you growing in your faith?

JUNE 18

PRESENCE OF GOD

TODAY'S PROMISE

Because of Christ and our faith in him, we can now come boldly and confidently into God's presence.

—EPHESIANS 3:12

TODAY'S THOUGHT

A holy God cannot be in the presence of sin, so how can a sinful person go boldly into God's presence? Only through Jesus Christ's life, death, and resurrection, and your faith in him. If you have asked Jesus to forgive your sins, you are now holy and blameless as far as God is concerned. He sees you as if you have never sinned, and he welcomes you into a relationship with him. You can come into his presence with boldness and confidence.

TODAY'S PLAN

Do you have what it takes—faith in Jesus—to be in God's presence?

FAILURE

TODAY'S PROMISE

Anyone who listens to my teaching and follows it is wise, like a person who builds a house on solid rock. Though the rain comes in torrents and the floodwaters rise and the winds beat against that house, it won't collapse because it is built on bedrock. But anyone who hears my teaching and doesn't obey it is foolish, like a person who builds a house on sand. When the rains and floods come and the winds beat against that house, it will collapse with a mighty crash. —MATTHEW 7:24-27

TODAY'S THOUGHT

Scripture reminds you to define success in terms of faithfulness to God. God will reward your faithfulness even if you fail in the eyes of the world. When you follow God's wisdom and his ways, your life will rest on a firm foundation that will last forever.

TODAY'S PLAN

How are you successful in God's eyes even if you feel like a failure right now?

GOD'S CARE

TODAY'S PROMISE

Give your burdens to the LORD, and he will take care of you. He will not permit the godly to slip and fall. —PSALM 55:22

TODAY'S THOUGHT

God cares for you and helps you whenever you ask. When you bring your burdens to God in prayer, you will experience freedom from worry and anxiety because you know he is listening and he cares. You can receive the assurance of God's love and concern through the promises of his Word and through prayer.

TODAY'S PLAN

How have you experienced God's care when you go to him in prayer?

DISCIPLINE

TODAY'S PROMISE

*No discipline is enjoyable while it is happening—
it's painful! But afterward there will be a peaceful
harvest of right living for those who are trained in
this way.* —HEBREWS 12:11

TODAY'S THOUGHT

The goal of discipline is to prevent you from
harming yourself and others, which also pro-
motes healthy relationships. Sin always damages
your relationship with God and others. God's
discipline is an act of love to keep you from
damaging your most important relationships and
to help you become the person he created you to
be. Left to yourself, you will tend to move away
from God and toward sin. God's discipline
reminds you of the right way to live. He
promises that the ultimate result of his discipline will be blessing.

TODAY'S PLAN

*Can you think of a time when God was disciplining you?
How did you grow from it?*

SATISFACTION

TODAY'S PROMISE

Those who drink the water I give will never be thirsty again. It becomes a fresh, bubbling spring within them, giving them eternal life.   —JOHN 4:14

TODAY'S THOUGHT

Everyone longs to be satisfied. Everyone is searching for something to quench their thirsting souls. But too many people try to fill their lives with the wrong things. The key is to fill yourself with something that will last. God promises that when you fill your heart and mind with his Word and his Spirit, you will be truly fulfilled and satisfied for all eternity.

TODAY'S PLAN

Where do you find true satisfaction?

FREEDOM

TODAY'S PROMISE

The LORD God placed the man in the Garden of Eden to tend and watch over it. But the LORD God warned him, "You may freely eat the fruit of every tree in the garden—except the tree of the knowledge of good and evil. If you eat its fruit, you are sure to die." —GENESIS 2:15-17

TODAY'S THOUGHT

Genuine love requires the freedom to choose. From the beginning, God desired a loving relationship with you, so he gave you this freedom. If he hadn't given us the freedom to choose, he would have created robots, not humans. But with the ability to make choices comes the possibility that you will choose your own way instead of God's way. Your own way always leads to sin, which breaks God's heart. But you can choose to do right by choosing to follow God's way. When you do so, God is greatly pleased.

TODAY'S PLAN

With your God-given freedom to choose, have you chosen God and his ways?

HOPE

TODAY'S PROMISE

We live with great expectation, and we have a priceless inheritance—an inheritance that is kept in heaven for you, pure and undefiled, beyond the reach of change and decay. And through your faith, God is protecting you by his power until you receive this salvation, which is ready to be revealed on the last day for all to see. So be truly glad. There is wonderful joy ahead, even though you have to endure many trials for a little while.

—1 PETER 1:3-6

TODAY'S THOUGHT

Just as focusing on a fixed point in the distance helps you move in a straight line, Jesus' followers must fix their eyes on heaven. As you move straight toward your goal, the hope you have for eternity will help you endure the discomforts and trials of daily life.

TODAY'S PLAN

How can the hope you have in Jesus keep you moving forward today?

CELEBRATION

TODAY'S PROMISE

In the same way, there is joy in the presence of God's angels when even one sinner repents. —LUKE 15:10

TODAY'S THOUGHT

Heaven is filled with celebrations too wonderful for the human mind to imagine. Angels worship God in mighty celebration and rejoice wildly when just one sinner repents. All believers will celebrate together at the great banquet of the Lord in heaven. Look forward to the day when you too will be able to join in these great heavenly events.

TODAY'S PLAN

How can you experience heavenly celebrations today while you are still on this earth?

LOVE

TODAY'S PROMISE

Those who accept my commandments and obey them are the ones who love me. And because they love me, my Father will love them. And I will love them and reveal myself to each of them. —JOHN 14:21

TODAY'S THOUGHT

Like a father with his child, God is delighted when you love him with all your heart and soul. He loves it when you imitate his character by displaying integrity, honesty, and purity of heart. When you obey God, it shows him that you love him enough to trust him with your life.

TODAY'S PLAN

Do you show your love for God by obeying his commandments?

CONSCIENCE

TODAY'S PROMISE

Cling to your faith in Christ, and keep your conscience clear. For some people have deliberately violated their consciences; as a result, their faith has been shipwrecked. —1 TIMOTHY 1:19

TODAY'S THOUGHT

God's Word says that if you ignore your conscience, your faith will be shipwrecked. When you sin, you are deliberately going against your conscience. You know what you are doing is wrong because your conscience tells you it is, but you do it anyway because sin is often so appealing. If you continually do what your conscience tells you not to, eventually you will no longer hear it warning you of danger. Without a strong conscience, you become desensitized to sin and your heart becomes hardened. The key to a healthy conscience is faith in Jesus Christ.

TODAY'S PLAN

Have you been listening to your conscience or ignoring it? Your answer may be an indication of the condition of your faith.

HUMILITY

TODAY'S PROMISE

Humble yourselves before the Lord, and he will lift you up in honor.

—JAMES 4:10

TODAY'S THOUGHT

You must be humble in order to recognize the sin in your life. Pride gives the devil the key to your heart, but humility changes the lock and gives God the key. Replace any pride you may have with the humility that comes from godly sorrow over your sin. Openly admit that you need God, and seek his forgiveness. Only a humble person is able to do this. When you do, God promises to bless you with honor.

TODAY'S PLAN

If you are truly sorry for your sins, you know you are developing a humble heart.

EXAMPLE

TODAY'S PROMISE

Take a new grip with your tired hands and strengthen your weak knees. Mark out a straight path for your feet so that those who are weak and lame will not fall but become strong.
—HEBREWS 12:12-13

TODAY'S THOUGHT

Everyone models *something* to *someone*. At times we all follow the example of someone else, and likewise we all set an example for others. The Bible promises that the way you live will influence others, and not just in matters of daily living. You can influence others for good or evil, for Christ or Satan. What kind of example have you been setting for others lately?

TODAY'S PLAN

How can your daily life set an example for others that will make them want to believe in Jesus?

HEAVEN

TODAY'S PROMISE

God blesses those who are poor and realize their need for him, for the Kingdom of Heaven is theirs.

—MATTHEW 5:3

TODAY'S THOUGHT

If you believe Jesus died to take the punishment for your sins and you recognize that only he can forgive you, the Bible promises you will go to heaven. You cannot earn your way to heaven; it is God's gift to those who admit their need for Jesus.

TODAY'S PLAN

Are you sure that you will go to heaven?

JULY

ENCOURAGEMENT

TODAY'S PROMISE

As soon as I pray, you answer me; you encourage me by giving me strength. —PSALM 138:3

TODAY'S THOUGHT

Looking at your circumstances instead of focusing on God can bring discouragement. It's easy to focus on the problem in front of you instead of seeing that God is standing by to help you overcome it. Don't let your feelings of discouragement cause you to doubt God's love for you; that will only draw you away from your greatest source of help. Be encouraged instead that God gives you strength and helps you succeed as you trust in him. Run to God in prayer; he promises to hear, answer, and encourage you.

TODAY'S PLAN

When you are feeling discouraged, where do you turn for help and encouragement?

HONESTY

TODAY'S PROMISE

Who may climb the mountain of the LORD? Who may stand in his holy place? Only those whose hands and hearts are pure, who . . . never tell lies. They will receive the LORD's blessing and have a right relationship with God their savior.

—PSALM 24:3-5

TODAY'S THOUGHT

God requires honesty because honesty shows purity, integrity, and a desire to do what is true and right. Honesty creates trust, and trust is the basis of all relationships. God wants you to be completely honest—with him, with yourself, and with others. You do not honor God if you cheat or take advantage of others to get ahead. When you are honest in even the smallest details, you gain some distinct advantages: a clear conscience, the trust and respect of others, and God's blessing. Determine today to never tell lies.

TODAY'S PLAN

Would your closest friends describe you as an honest person?

NEIGHBORS

TODAY'S PROMISE

Be careful to live properly among your unbelieving neighbors. Then even if they accuse you of doing wrong, they will see your honorable behavior, and they will give honor to God when he judges the world.

—1 PETER 2:12

TODAY'S THOUGHT

Treat your neighbors, especially unbelievers, with love and respect, integrity and graciousness. Be an example of godliness, even if they treat you poorly or unfairly. If they don't know God, see it as an opportunity to witness to your faith. Perhaps you will win them over through friendship and the love of God that is shining through you.

TODAY'S PLAN

How can you show God's love to your neighbor today?

OUR NATION

TODAY'S PROMISE

I urge you, first of all, to pray for all people. Ask God to help them; intercede on their behalf, and give thanks for them. Pray this way for kings and all who are in authority so that we can live peaceful and quiet lives marked by godliness and dignity.

—1 TIMOTHY 2:1-2

TODAY'S THOUGHT

It's important for Christians to pray for our nation because the Bible says it leads to peace. Pray for this nation to be protected by God's mighty hand. Pray for its leaders to be humble and wise, to discern right from wrong, and to champion the cause of the needy and helpless. A nation that allows or endorses immorality is subject to judgment and will eventually collapse from the inside out. A nation that collectively worships the one true God will stand firm and live in peace.

TODAY'S PLAN

How can you pray for your country today?

HEALING

TODAY'S PROMISE

He personally carried our sins in his body on the cross so that we can be dead to sin and live for what is right. By his wounds you are healed. —1 PETER 2:24

TODAY'S THOUGHT

A congenital disease is raging within you all the time—it is called sin. Sin is a disease that takes not only a physical, mental, and emotional toll, but also a spiritual one. When you come to Jesus to treat this disease, he promises healing through the antidote of forgiveness. When you ask him, Jesus forgives your sin. A miraculous healing takes place, and this disease can no longer control the way you live.

TODAY'S PLAN

Have you asked God for the medicine of forgiveness to heal your worst sickness?

DIVERSITY

TODAY'S PROMISE

We are many parts of one body, and we all belong to each other. In his grace, God has given us different gifts for doing certain things well. —ROMANS 12:5-6

TODAY'S THOUGHT

Just as all kinds of instruments are necessary to make up an orchestra, so all kinds of gifts and perspectives are needed to make up an effective group of people such as the church. In fact, God promises that he has specifically given you a unique gift so that you can do something well in the work of his Kingdom. Then God puts people with different gifts together so that their gifts can complement each other. It is actually through diversity that the most progress can be made. If everyone thought the same way or did the same things, the status quo would never change and little would get done.

TODAY'S PLAN

Have you discovered the unique gift God has given you? How is it different from those around you yet equally important?

JUDGING OTHERS

TODAY'S PROMISE

Do not judge others, and you will not be judged. For you will be treated as you treat others. The standard you use in judging is the standard by which you will be judged.

— MATTHEW 7:1-2

TODAY'S THOUGHT

Be careful not to judge other people because you may not know all the facts of their circumstances. Just as you would not want others to hastily or unfairly evaluate you, refrain from doing it to others. Before you jump to conclusions about someone, it helps to remember the hurts you've experienced when others wrongly judged you. This will broaden your perspective and help you avoid looking at other people through a negative filter that distorts their reputation. See others as Jesus sees them—as God's children worthy of love and kindness— and replace judgment with mercy.

TODAY'S PLAN

Do you notice someone's negative or positive qualities first? Your answer is an indicator of how quick you are to judge others.

QUIET

TODAY'S PROMISE

When you pray, go away by yourself, shut the door behind you, and pray to your Father in private. Then your Father, who sees everything, will reward you.
　　　　　　　　　　　　　　　　—MATTHEW 6:6

TODAY'S THOUGHT

Sometimes you must be still, quiet, and alone to hear God speak. Sometimes you must simply spend time in his presence without even verbalizing your prayers. Just find a quiet place and tell God you are listening and ready to hear him speak to your heart and mind. He promises to see you and reward you.

TODAY'S PLAN

When was the last time you were quiet before God?

SUCCESS

TODAY'S PROMISE

Be strong and very courageous. Be careful to obey all the instructions Moses gave you. Do not deviate from them, turning either to the right or to the left. Then you will be successful in everything you do.

—JOSHUA 1:7

TODAY'S THOUGHT

The Bible is the Word of God and the wisdom of God. It has both useful instruction and spiritual power to help you deal with any challenge. The key to success is found in commitment to obedience. So challenge yourself to obey God's Word, and you will enjoy success as God defines it—and that is the only kind of success that is truly worth achieving.

TODAY'S PLAN

Do you believe you can enjoy success by committing to obey God's Word?

LISTENING

TODAY'S PROMISE

Come and listen to my counsel. I'll share my heart with you and make you wise. —PROVERBS 1:23

TODAY'S THOUGHT

God promises that if you listen to him, you will become wise. There are three ways you can listen to God: (1) Pray. Prayer is not just talking to God; it is also listening to him talk to you. (2) Read the Bible. God's Word is your instruction manual for living. In it you will find advice and wisdom about how the world works and how to apply this knowledge to life. (3) Listen to godly advice. Those who have gone before you and gained wisdom can share it with you, saving you much pain and heartache.

TODAY'S PLAN

What can you do this week to listen to God?

JULY 11

HELP

TODAY'S PROMISE

The LORD is my strength and shield. I trust him with all my heart. He helps me, and my heart is filled with joy.

—PSALM 28:7

TODAY'S THOUGHT

When you ask God for help and trust that he will help, you open a lifeline to the God who loves to do the impossible for you. If you trust him wholeheartedly, he will help you in all that you ask. You will be filled with joy when you see the amazing things God has planned for you!

TODAY'S PLAN

How can you trust that God will help you?

ASSURANCE

TODAY'S PROMISE

Through Christ you have come to trust in God. And you have placed your faith and hope in God because he raised Christ from the dead and gave him great glory. —1 PETER 1:21

TODAY'S THOUGHT

Trust is an essential ingredient in any good relationship. When you trust someone, you can be absolutely sure of that person. But no human being is completely trustworthy because no one is perfect. Only God can be totally trusted without fear of disappointment. You can be assured that what he says is true and what he does is reliable. He has never broken a single one of his promises, so you can be sure his promises for the future will be fulfilled too. People are not perfect, and they will sometimes fail you. God is perfect, and he will never fail you. The world is full of uncertainty, but you can have assurance because God keeps his promises.

TODAY'S PLAN

How will your trust in God and your assurance of his promises impact your relationship with him today?

OVERWHELMED

TODAY'S PROMISE

O LORD, I have so many enemies; so many are
against me. . . . But you, O LORD, are a shield
around me; you are my glory, the one who holds my
head high. . . . Victory comes from you, O LORD.

—PSALM 3:1, 3, 8

TODAY'S THOUGHT

The powers of evil can seem overwhelming
at times. You may wonder how you can keep
going. But God says not to be afraid because
he will act like a shield around you. When you
are afraid, the courage you need comes only from
realizing how powerful God is. Then the odds
won't seem so impossible. No enemy can stand
before him. God is more powerful than any
force against you.

TODAY'S PLAN

Are you feeling overwhelmed? How can you trust God for
victory?

DISASTER

TODAY'S PROMISE

The LORD himself, the King of Israel, will live among you! At last your troubles will be over, and you will never again fear disaster. —ZEPHANIAH 3:15

TODAY'S THOUGHT

When disaster strikes, do not doubt God's good intentions for you. The wonder of creation, the evidence of God's constant care in your life, and the priceless gift of Jesus Christ to save you can give you confidence that God will help and guide you when you trust in him. Even in the face of disaster, you can take comfort in God's promise that one day you will never have to fear disaster again.

TODAY'S PLAN

What would it be like to never experience the fear of disaster?

FOLLOWING

TODAY'S PROMISE

[Jesus said,] "If you do not carry your own cross and follow me, you cannot be my disciple." —LUKE 14:27

TODAY'S THOUGHT

Following Jesus is a costly commitment. It means leaving behind everything that might take your focus off him and devoting yourself to him with all your heart. It will be easier to follow Jesus when you think less about what you are giving up and more about the blessings and benefits that come from life with him.

TODAY'S PLAN

Are you following Jesus closely, or are you beginning to lag behind?

COMPROMISE

TODAY'S PROMISE

Be very careful never to make a treaty with the people who live in the land where you are going. If you do, you will follow their evil ways and be trapped. —EXODUS 34:12

TODAY'S THOUGHT

This warning points out the danger of falling into a lifestyle of sin. The laws of society make you pay a fine or go to prison when you commit a crime because of the recognition that certain behaviors harm others. If those behaviors are left unchecked, rebellion and chaos will reign. God knows that certain behaviors not only harm you physically but also put your soul in mortal danger. That is why God warns you not to compromise with the evil that surrounds you. If you do, you will soon be living comfortably with sin rather than struggling to be true to God and his Word.

TODAY'S PLAN

How can you live in today's world without compromising your faith?

MEANING

TODAY'S PROMISE

You will show me the way of life, granting me the joy of your presence and the pleasures of living with you forever.

—PSALM 16:11

TODAY'S THOUGHT

A primary cause of despair is the feeling that life is ultimately meaningless. Why keep going if nothing really matters? Conversely, the sense that life has meaning gives a person energy, purpose, and resilience, even in the midst of trials. The Bible reveals the deepest reasons for your existence, supplying compelling incentives to persevere and overcome your despair to reach a glorious future that will be well worth the effort.

God's Word is full of his promises to reveal to you the purpose for which you were created.

TODAY'S PLAN

Where do you find the meaning of your life?

COMFORT

TODAY'S PROMISE

Even when I walk through the darkest valley, I will not be afraid, for you are close beside me. Your rod and your staff protect and comfort me. —PSALM 23:4

TODAY'S THOUGHT

Intimacy with God helps you see his personal touch in your life every day. He is your creator and shepherd. He wants to communicate with you, watch out for you, care for you, advise you, and give you his joy and blessings. You must walk with him as he guides you step-by-step. When you stay close to him, he will comfort and protect you. Look for him in your life today, and you will see him right there beside you.

TODAY'S PLAN

In what way can you draw closer to God and experience his comfort?

PROBLEMS

TODAY'S PROMISE

[Jesus said,] "Here on earth you will have many trials and sorrows. But take heart, because I have overcome the world."
—JOHN 16:33

TODAY'S THOUGHT

Perhaps the best way God helps you deal with problems is by guaranteeing a place in the future where there will be no problems. Human beings have made a mess of this world because of their sin. But no matter what your future on this earth holds, you can be sure that heaven will be free of problems and worries. Jesus guarantees that you'll have problems in this world, but he promises that you'll have none in the next.

TODAY'S PLAN

How can you look forward to a world without problems instead of being overwhelmed by the problems in this world?

FUTURE

TODAY'S PROMISE

When the Great Shepherd appears, you will receive a crown of never-ending glory and honor. . . . In his kindness God called you to share in his eternal glory by means of Christ Jesus. So after you have suffered a little while, he will restore, support, and strengthen you, and he will place you on a firm foundation. —1 PETER 5:4, 10

TODAY'S THOUGHT

As a heaven-bound follower of Jesus, try to put the present and the future in perspective. Here on earth, you will probably live for less than a hundred years. In heaven, one hundred *million* years will be just the beginning. If you are going to spend most of your time in heaven, you should spend your time here on earth preparing yourself to live there. When you have the right perspective on the future, you will live today with the right priorities.

TODAY'S PLAN

What can you do today to prepare for your glorious future in heaven?

BELONGING

TODAY'S PROMISE

What blessings await you when people hate you and exclude you and mock you and curse you as evil because you follow the Son of Man. —LUKE 6:22

TODAY'S THOUGHT

Consider your status as an outsider here on earth to be a blessing rather than a curse. You can look forward to receiving God's eternal blessing for the ridicule you endure today. As a Christian, you do not belong in this world—your real home is in heaven. Other believers are outsiders like you. Their friendship and accountability can encourage you to humbly and faithfully obey God. Then God promises you will reach the place where you truly belong.

TODAY'S PLAN

Where can you turn for comfort when you feel you don't belong here?

GOSSIP

TODAY'S PROMISE

If you claim to be religious but don't control your tongue, you are fooling yourself, and your religion is worthless.
—JAMES 1:26

TODAY'S THOUGHT

What comes out of your mouth shows what is in your heart. Your words show what kind of person you really are. Gossip, criticism, flattery, lying, and profanity are not only word problems but heart problems as well. Simply trying to control your words isn't enough. First you need a change of heart; then good, kind, and healing words will follow.

TODAY'S PLAN

How can you change your words today by first changing your heart?

RIGHTEOUSNESS

TODAY'S PROMISE

This Good News tells us how God makes us right in his sight. This is accomplished from start to finish by faith. As the Scriptures say, "It is through faith that a righteous person has life." —ROMANS 1:17

TODAY'S THOUGHT

Righteousness is consistently following God's Word and his will, being forgiven of your sins, walking with God daily, having an unwavering faith in God and his promises, loving him deeply, demonstrating persistent integrity, and avoiding evil. When you have faith and live in this way, God calls you righteous and promises to give you life.

TODAY'S PLAN

How can you be righteous in God's sight?

ADVICE

TODAY'S PROMISE

To those who listen to my teaching, more understanding will be given, and they will have an abundance of knowledge. —MATTHEW 13:12

TODAY'S THOUGHT

In an age of conflicting claims and confusing information, everyone is looking for wise counsel. Maybe that's why counselors are in such great demand and advice columnists are in every newspaper. But there is a critical difference between worldly advice and wise counsel. God's wisdom is best because he is all-knowing. Seek knowledge and understanding from the One who knows everything that will happen today and tomorrow and every day to come. Then you will have the wisdom to weigh and interpret advice from others.

TODAY'S PLAN

How can you make it a habit to seek advice first from God's Word?

MONEY

TODAY'S PROMISE

Those who love money will never have enough. How meaningless to think that wealth brings true happiness!
—ECCLESIASTES 5:10

TODAY'S THOUGHT

The pursuit of money and possessions can easily deceive you into thinking that if only you had a little more, you would be content. The Bible promises that nothing could be further from the truth. The desire for more always leads to discontent. Contentment comes not from material wealth but from spiritual wealth, so focus on making spiritual investments. The love of money and material things becomes a trap because it chains you to this earth. Your only hope of escape is to keep an eternal perspective and realize that true happiness is found not in earthly possessions but in your relationship with God.

TODAY'S PLAN

Have you fallen into the trap of believing that money will bring you happiness?

SIGNIFICANCE

TODAY'S PROMISE

What is the price of two sparrows—one copper coin? But not a single sparrow can fall to the ground without your Father knowing it. . . . So don't be afraid; you are more valuable to God than a whole flock of sparrows.

—MATTHEW 10:29-31

TODAY'S THOUGHT

Deep within every human heart lies a hunger for significance. We want our lives to count, to make a difference, to be worth something. Yet many people carry deep feelings of insignificance. Their lives are dominated not by their abilities but their inabilities. Everywhere they look they see others who are more successful, more gifted, more this or that. The Bible, however, says that every person has great value. You are significant, not because of anything you can accomplish on your own but because God loves you and promises that you are valuable to him.

TODAY'S PLAN

How does knowing that God values you increase your feelings of significance?

COMPASSION

TODAY'S PROMISE

The LORD is like a father to his children, tender and compassionate to those who fear him. —PSALM 103:13

TODAY'S THOUGHT

God shows his compassion to you by caring for you, providing for you, loving you, and blessing you. When you fear and obey him, he forgives your sins and restores your relationship with him.

TODAY'S PLAN

How can you show others the same compassion God shows you?

REWARDS

No eye has seen, no ear has heard, and no mind has imagined what God has prepared for those who love him.

—1 CORINTHIANS 2:9

If Christians suffer like everybody else, why bother living for God or following him? If all we had to live for were the rewards of this life, then a "why bother" attitude might be understandable. But this perspective is wrong for at least two reasons: First, when you try to obey God, your relationships are fulfilling, your life displays integrity, and your conscience is clear. Second, this life is not all there is. The Bible is clear that those who trust Jesus Christ for salvation and the forgiveness of their sins receive the promise of eternal life. Your faithfulness may or may not result in rewards in this life, but your rewards in heaven will be greater than you can imagine.

Are you working only for rewards here on earth, or are you looking forward to the rewards God promises in heaven?

REPUTATION

TODAY'S PROMISE

Never let loyalty and kindness leave you! Tie them around your neck as a reminder. Write them deep within your heart. Then you will find favor with both God and people, and you will earn a good reputation.

—PROVERBS 3:3-4

TODAY'S THOUGHT

Everyone has a reputation. Whether you intentionally try to project a certain image or you couldn't care less what others think, people still form an opinion of you based on your personality, your character, your behavior, and your abilities. A good reputation can help you make friends and gain respect. A bad reputation can attract others of ill repute to you, or it can leave you isolated, shunned, and disrespected. God promises you will earn a good reputation when you show kindness, loyalty, and love to your neighbors.

TODAY'S PLAN

What kind of reputation are you earning?

CONFIDENCE

TODAY'S PROMISE

Let us who live in the light be clearheaded, protected by the armor of faith and love, and wearing as our helmet the confidence of our salvation.

—1 THESSALONIANS 5:8

TODAY'S THOUGHT

Many great athletes say that the biggest obstacle to winning is mental, not physical. It's the same way in your spiritual life. Your confidence does not come from your physical circumstances—how you look or what you achieve. Rather, it comes from faith—the inner assurance that God is by your side, daily protecting you, fighting for you, and winning the victories in your life for you.

TODAY'S PLAN

What can you do to increase your confidence that God is actively involved in your life?

OBEDIENCE

TODAY'S PROMISE

Do what is right and good in the LORD's sight, so all will go well with you.   —DEUTERONOMY 6:18

TODAY'S THOUGHT

The right thing to do is the smart thing to do. God's commandments are not burdensome obligations but pathways to joyful, meaningful, satisfying lives. God's demand for obedience comes out of his desire for your well-being. Since God is the Creator of life, he knows how life is best lived. Obedience demonstrates your willingness to follow through on what God says to do. Obedience shows how much you trust that God's way is best for you.

TODAY'S PLAN

Do you see obedience as a burden or as a pathway to the best life?

AUGUST

NOURISHMENT

TODAY'S PROMISE

Jesus replied, "I am the bread of life. Whoever comes to me will never be hungry again. Whoever believes in me will never be thirsty." —JOHN 6:35

TODAY'S THOUGHT

Jesus is the spiritual nourishment your soul craves. He truly satisfies your deepest spiritual hunger by his daily presence. He meets your needs, works good in your life, carries out his plans for you, and offers you peace of mind and the promise of eternal life. Feed your soul with Jesus, and you will be satisfied for eternity.

TODAY'S PLAN

How can you satisfy your soul today?

HOLY SPIRIT

TODAY'S PROMISE

When you believed in Christ, he identified you as his own by giving you the Holy Spirit, whom he promised long ago. The Spirit is God's guarantee that he will give us the inheritance he promised and that he has purchased us to be his own people. He did this so we would praise and glorify him.

—EPHESIANS 1:13–14

TODAY'S THOUGHT

God gives you the Holy Spirit when you believe in Jesus Christ. In fact, it is through the promptings of the Holy Spirit that you are able to believe in Christ. Because the Holy Spirit lives in you, you can pray expectantly that God will release the Spirit's power in your life. God fulfilled his promise to send the Holy Spirit, and the Holy Spirit assures us that his promises for the future will also be fulfilled.

TODAY'S PLAN

Ask the Holy Spirit to release his power in you to help you live more like Jesus each day.

HEART

TODAY'S PROMISE

I will give you a new heart, and I will put a new spirit in you. I will take out your stony, stubborn heart and give you a tender, responsive heart.

—EZEKIEL 36:26

TODAY'S THOUGHT

When you give God control of your life, he gives you a new heart, a new nature, and a new desire to please him. God renews your heart when you humble yourself before him, turn away from sinful habits, and make a daily effort to connect with him. As you do these things, your love for God will grow. He changes even the coldest heart of stone into an obedient and loving heart. Are you willing to let him change you?

TODAY'S PLAN

Have you asked God to change your heart?

JOY

TODAY'S PROMISE

The joy of the LORD is your strength! —NEHEMIAH 8:10

TODAY'S THOUGHT

Joy springs from God's love, which is not dependent on your circumstances or your performance. When you realize just how great God's love for you really is, you become less vulnerable to depression and despair over problems and disappointments. The more you love him, know him, walk with him, and become like him, the greater your joy will be. You will find perfect and lasting joy in heaven, but you can experience joy now by walking with God.

TODAY'S PLAN

Does the thought of God's great love for you bring you joy?

PEACE

TODAY'S PROMISE

The LORD gives his people strength. The LORD blesses them with peace.   —PSALM 29:11

TODAY'S THOUGHT

Peace with God comes from living the way God wants his people to live. That happens when you develop a relationship with him and live according to the standards he gives in his Word, the Bible. Then God strengthens you and blesses you with the peace that is found only in him.

TODAY'S PLAN

How can you experience the blessing of God's peace today?

MATURITY

TODAY'S PROMISE

God, who began the good work within you, will continue his work until it is finally finished on the day when Christ Jesus returns. . . . Looking forward to what lies ahead, I press on to reach the end of the race and receive the heavenly prize for which God, through Christ Jesus, is calling us.

—PHILIPPIANS 1:6; 3:13-14

TODAY'S THOUGHT

The Bible describes spiritual maturity as completing a task or reaching the finish line. We should mature in character to become exemplary and productive people. We should mature in faith, striving for and reaching the spiritual goals God sets for us. Maturity is reaching the finish lines of life and finishing well.

TODAY'S PLAN

Have you set any goals for spiritual maturity? If not, study the Bible to discover what you should be striving for.

CONSEQUENCES

TODAY'S PROMISE

Those who live only to satisfy their own sinful nature will harvest decay and death from that sinful nature. But those who live to please the Spirit will harvest everlasting life from the Spirit. —GALATIANS 6:8

TODAY'S THOUGHT

A gun fires, a bullet flies, and a person in its path dies. That death is the consequence of someone's pulling the trigger of a loaded weapon. Similarly, hurtful words may wound someone else. On the other hand, helpful words may lead a person to Christ. In both cases, the words have consequences. Sin always has negative consequences, but faithfulness to God always has positive consequences. Focus on doing things that have positive consequences, and you will have less time to act in ways that have negative consequences.

TODAY'S PLAN

Have your actions lately had more negative consequences or more positive consequences?

PAIN

TODAY'S PROMISE

The LORD nurses them when they are sick and restores them to health. —PSALM 41:3

TODAY'S THOUGHT

God can heal any pain, whether a broken body or a broken heart. As you wait for God to fulfill his promise to heal you, either in this life or in heaven, don't give up. Believe that one day he can and will take away all your pain and fully restore you. Until then, he will give you the strength to keep going.

TODAY'S PLAN

What is the source of your pain today? Have you asked God to heal and restore you?

FEAR

TODAY'S PROMISE

God is our refuge and strength, always ready to help in times of trouble. So we will not fear when earthquakes come and the mountains crumble into the sea.

—PSALM 46:1-2

TODAY'S THOUGHT

God is greater than the most severe threats to your life. When you recognize that sin has corrupted this world, you will no longer be surprised or overcome by the troubles you see. Ask God to stay close by your side. He promises to comfort you and give you the confident assurance that he is with you in every circumstance. He promises that he will always be ready to help you when you are afraid.

TODAY'S PLAN

When you are overcome with fear, how do you draw closer to God?

HOLINESS

TODAY'S PROMISE

Work at living in peace with everyone, and work at living a holy life, for those who are not holy will not see the Lord. —HEBREWS 12:14

TODAY'S THOUGHT

Holiness is an indicator of the health of your relationship with God. Being holy includes trying your best to treat others with the same mercy and unconditional love that God would show them—and that God has showed you. You won't achieve perfect holiness in this life, but God asks that you sincerely try to be more like him each day. The more you understand what the Holy One has done for you, the more you will want to live the holy life he desires.

TODAY'S PLAN

How can you live out God's peace and holiness in your relationships with others?

INTEGRITY

TODAY'S PROMISE

The LORD rewarded me for doing right. He has seen my innocence. To the faithful you show yourself faithful; to those with integrity you show integrity.

—PSALM 18:24-25

TODAY'S THOUGHT

Integrity allows you to experience uninterrupted fellowship with God and helps you live under his protection and guidance. When you lack integrity, you are exposed to all kinds of sin and danger, including the disintegration of your character. But when you show integrity by doing the right thing and remaining innocent of sin, God promises to be faithful and reward you.

TODAY'S PLAN

How has God rewarded you for your integrity?

ABILITIES

TODAY'S PROMISE

He takes no pleasure in the strength of a horse or in human might. No, the LORD's delight is in those who fear him, those who put their hope in his unfailing love. —PSALM 147:10-11

TODAY'S THOUGHT

God is more impressed by your faith than your abilities. He uses your abilities in proportion to your faith. If you want to delight God, say yes to him, step out in faith, and watch him accomplish great things through you. Abilities give you the potential to do good; faith gives you the power to do good. Neither potential nor power alone is sufficient—they must work in harmony.

TODAY'S PLAN

Do you have more faith in your own abilities than you do in God? Try putting your limited abilities to work with an unlimited faith in God.

SPIRITUAL WARFARE

TODAY'S PROMISE

Watch out for your great enemy, the devil. He prowls around like a roaring lion, looking for someone to devour. Stand firm against him, and be strong in your faith. . . . After you have suffered a little while, he will restore, support, and strengthen you, and he will place you on a firm foundation.

—1 PETER 5:8-10

TODAY'S THOUGHT

The goal of the forces of evil is to defy God and to wear down believers until they are led into sin. This gives Satan pleasure, and it increases his power on earth. Therefore you must always be alert for both the sneak attacks and the frontal assaults of the evil one. Eventually God will destroy the powers of evil for all time. Until that day, however, you must fight and overcome evil by standing firm in your faith in God.

TODAY'S PLAN

How can I fight the forces of evil in my life?

IMPOSSIBILITY

TODAY'S PROMISE

Jesus looked at them intently and said, "Humanly speaking, it is impossible. But with God everything is possible."   —MATTHEW 19:26

TODAY'S THOUGHT

There should be no doubt that God specializes in doing what from a human perspective is impossible. But the end of your abilities is the beginning of his. The God who spoke all creation into being can do the impossible for you. You must believe that he can and that he wants to. When you try to cope with problems in your own strength, you easily become overwhelmed. When you focus on God, you become aware of his power at work in your life. You can cope with impossible situations when God's strength replaces your weakness. Then your impossibilities will become God's opportunities.

TODAY'S PLAN

How might God turn your most impossible problem into an opportunity to do something great in your life?

JUSTICE

TODAY'S PROMISE

If you do what is wrong, you will be paid back for the wrong you have done. For God has no favorites.

—COLOSSIANS 3:25

TODAY'S THOUGHT

Don't be so quick to beg God for justice. Then he just might have to punish you too. Instead, beg God for his love so he will forgive you. Don't be so quick to beg God for fairness, because he might end up taking away what you have. Instead, beg for mercy so you can be saved from the judgment that all people deserve. Because of Christ, God's justice allows him to grant mercy to those whose hearts sincerely love him.

TODAY'S PLAN

Would you rather have complete justice or God's mercy in eternity?

BROKENNESS

TODAY'S PROMISE

I will bless those who have humble and contrite hearts, who tremble at my word. —ISAIAH 66:2

TODAY'S THOUGHT

Humility is a form of brokenness, which you experience when you realize that you cannot fix or control everything that happens to you. Acknowledging your dependence on God allows him to help you with all your needs and problems. He promises to bless you in your vulnerability.

TODAY'S PLAN

Do you maintain your humility before God in the midst of brokenness? How might God bless you by meeting your needs today?

MOTIVES

TODAY'S PROMISE

Pay careful attention to your own work, for then you will get the satisfaction of a job well done, and you won't need to compare yourself to anyone else.

—GALATIANS 6:4

TODAY'S THOUGHT

People often get stressed out when they take on activities and responsibilities for the wrong reasons. As you consider upcoming involvements, ask God to help you do things with the right motives and to reveal any motives that might be unhealthy. Then you will be better able to decide which activities you should commit to and which ones you should say no to. When you say yes with the right motives, you will be able to work with passion and purpose, which will give you great satisfaction and fulfillment.

TODAY'S PLAN

Are you saying yes with the right motives?

FAITHFULNESS

TODAY'S PROMISE

The LORD rewarded me for doing right. He has seen my innocence. To the faithful you show yourself faithful; to those with integrity you show integrity. To the pure you show yourself pure, but to the wicked you show yourself hostile. —2 SAMUEL 22:25-27

TODAY'S THOUGHT

Faithfulness says, "You can count on me—I will never let you down." Husbands and wives vow on their wedding day to be faithful to one another, to be devoted and committed to each other, to stay together no matter what. Throughout the Bible, God shows that faithfulness is one of his foundational qualities. There is nothing like the faithfulness of another to build your sense of security in your relationship with that person. And there is nothing like the faithfulness of God to build your confidence in your eternal security.

TODAY'S PLAN

How can you experience the rewards of faithfulness?

ABILITIES

TODAY'S PROMISE

Then the LORD asked Moses, "Who makes a person's mouth? Who decides whether people speak or do not speak, hear or do not hear, see or do not see? Is it not I, the LORD? Now go! I will be with you as you speak, and I will instruct you in what to say."

—EXODUS 4:11-12

TODAY'S THOUGHT

When God asks you to do something, he gives you the abilities and the extra resources you need to get the job done. Moses didn't think he had the power of persuasion to confront Pharaoh on behalf of God's people, but God promised to be with him and to give him the words to say. Even when you think you cannot accomplish the task God has put before you, remember that he is with you and he will give you what you need to carry out his will.

TODAY'S PLAN

What is God asking you to do for him? What specific abilities has he given you to fulfill that purpose?

MISTAKES

TODAY'S PROMISE

Fools think their own way is right, but the wise listen to others. —PROVERBS 12:15

TODAY'S THOUGHT

The Bible promises that rejecting wise advice will lead to mistakes. Good words and actions are the result of good thoughts and character. When you spend time meditating on what is good and right and listening to those who are good and wise, your words and actions will be good, right, and wise, and you will avoid many mistakes.

TODAY'S PLAN

What mistakes have you avoided by listening to good advice from someone else?

AUGUST 21

DECISIONS

TODAY'S PROMISE

*Your commands make me wiser than my enemies,
for they are my constant guide.*   —PSALM 119:98

TODAY'S THOUGHT

When you ask God to give you wisdom, perspective, and a desire to obey him, he promises to do it. The more you get to know God through prayer and reading the Bible, the more you know what God wants you to do. And when you know what God wants you to do, you can make the right decisions when you are faced with difficult choices. God's will becomes clear as you are guided by his Word.

TODAY'S PLAN

Are you using the Bible, God's Word, as your guide for decision making?

MONEY

TODAY'S PROMISE

Honor the LORD with your wealth and with the best part of everything you produce. Then he will fill your barns with grain, and your vats will overflow with good wine. —PROVERBS 3:9-10

TODAY'S THOUGHT

Instead of viewing money as yours to use as you wish, see it as God's to use as he wishes. Giving the first part of everything you receive back to God will help you maintain this perspective, and God promises to bless you for it.

TODAY'S PLAN

Do you give God first priority when it comes to your money? If not, what can you do to change that?

GOALS

TODAY'S PROMISE

Take delight in the LORD, and he will give you your heart's desires.
—PSALM 37:4

TODAY'S THOUGHT

Before a ship sets out on a long voyage, the captain needs to plot the course. This includes choosing the route, setting the schedule, determining the places to stop, and deciding the responsibilities for each crew member. By planning ahead and setting attainable goals, the captain ensures that the ship will stay on the right track and arrive safely at its destination. The same principle is true for you. Setting attainable goals is necessary for determining your destination and your course for getting there. Without goals, you would wander aimlessly through life. When God is your captain and plots your life's journey according to his plan for you, you will stay on track and arrive safely at your ultimate destination—heaven.

TODAY'S PLAN

How can you align your goals with God's direction for your life?

DISAPPOINTMENT

TODAY'S PROMISE

They cried out to you and were saved. They trusted in you and were never disgraced. —PSALM 22:5

TODAY'S THOUGHT

The truth is that life is full of disappointment for us. On the other hand, we often disappoint God because of our sins. But God doesn't want us to dwell on what could have been. He is the God of hope and wants us to focus on what can be. That's why he sent his Son, Jesus, to take the punishment for your disappointing behavior so that you can stand before him as more than good enough. You are actually holy in his eyes. The next time you feel disappointed, remember everything God has done for you. Use this time to grow, and take comfort that you have the approval of the only One who really matters.

TODAY'S PLAN

Knowing that God loves you and turns bad into good, how can you now move past your disappointment?

REGRETS

TODAY'S PROMISE

Oh, what joy for those whose disobedience is forgiven, whose sins are put out of sight. Yes, what joy for those whose record the LORD has cleared of sin.

—ROMANS 4:7-8

TODAY'S THOUGHT

Guilt is a legitimate spiritual response to sin; regret is sorrow over the consequences of our decisions, both the sinful and the simply unfortunate. While God promises to remove the guilt of all who seek his forgiveness, he does not prevent the consequences of your sin. It is most likely the regret over those consequences that you still carry, that weighs you down with remorse. God promises to help you deal with your regret so you can move into the future without that heavy burden. He completely gets rid of your sin; don't take it back by hanging on to regrets.

TODAY'S PLAN

Are you still holding on to regrets over sins that God has forgiven?

BELONGING

TODAY'S PROMISE

Just as our bodies have many parts and each part has a special function, so it is with Christ's body. We are many parts of one body, and we all belong to each other. In his grace, God has given us different gifts for doing certain things well.

—ROMANS 12:4-6

TODAY'S THOUGHT

Belonging to God makes you part of Christ's body, the church. The next step is figuring out what part of the body you are. A hand that works? A foot that moves? Ears that listen? A mouth that speaks? When you learn what part you are, you have discovered your spiritual gift. And when you use that gift as God intended, you will find where you belong in the church, where you can best serve God and others, and where you feel a sense of purpose and fulfillment. When each person in the body understands what his or her part is and does it faithfully, the body functions as God intended.

TODAY'S PLAN

Where do you belong in the body of Christ?

CALL OF GOD

TODAY'S PROMISE

God's gifts and his call can never be withdrawn.

—ROMANS 11:29

TODAY'S THOUGHT

God's call is like your family name. Even when you feel you've dishonored your family, you do not lose your name. The same principle applies when you are a member of God's family. Because you are his child, God has given you specific gifts and called you to do certain tasks for him. If you don't use the gifts God has given you, he won't take them away but you will miss out on the best possible life he has planned for you. As long as you have life and breath, use your gifts to live out God's calling for your life—you can't lose.

TODAY'S PLAN

How can you begin to discover God's gifts and call in your life?

PRESENCE OF GOD

TODAY'S PROMISE

You go before me and follow me. You place your hand of blessing on my head. . . . I can never escape from your Spirit! I can never get away from your presence!
                                                     —PSALM 139:5-7

TODAY'S THOUGHT

The Bible, God's Word, promises that when you have a relationship with God, his presence is always with you. When you believe this promise, you will start to see events in your life as evidence of his presence with you. You will experience his love for you and receive his blessing.

TODAY'S PLAN

How often are you seeing God's presence in your life?

EVIL

TODAY'S PROMISE

Humble yourselves before God. Resist the devil, and he will flee from you.

—JAMES 4:7

TODAY'S THOUGHT

When you believe and live out the truths taught in God's Word, you will have the upper hand in the battle against evil. You must be humble before God and ask him for help. When you do this, he will give you discernment as well as protection against Satan and his demons, who continually fight for your soul. The Word of God and the power of the Holy Spirit are powerful resources that can help you resist your enemy. Stand strong and confident in your faith, and you can be sure that God will help you fight your battles and make you victorious.

TODAY'S PLAN

Humility helps you resist evil because it causes you to realize that you must rely on God's help. What specific temptation can you ask God to help you resist today?

GENEROSITY

TODAY'S PROMISE

"Bring all the tithes into the storehouse so there will be enough food in my Temple. If you do," says the Lord of Heaven's Armies, "I will open the windows of heaven for you. I will pour out a blessing so great you won't have enough room to take it in! Try it! Put me to the test!"
—MALACHI 3:10

TODAY'S THOUGHT

Old Testament law made it clear that God wanted his people to tithe—to give him the first tenth of their income. This demonstrated their obedience and trust that God would provide for them. When Jesus came, he made it clear that he loves a cheerful giver. This means that he loves it when you have a generous heart. Whatever the amount you give, you should honor the Lord with your wealth so that his work on earth can continue. God promises to bless you lavishly when you do this.

TODAY'S PLAN

Are you willing to step out in faith, give generously, and see how God blesses you?

MERCY

TODAY'S PROMISE

God blesses those who are merciful, for they will be shown mercy.
—MATTHEW 5:7

TODAY'S THOUGHT

Mercy can be defined as compassion poured out on needy people. But the mercy of God, which he expects us to model, goes one step further. God's mercy is undeserved favor. Even when you don't deserve mercy, he still extends it. Your sin and rebellion against God deserve his punishment. But instead of punishment, he promises you forgiveness and eternal life if you simply accept his mercy. Just as God has been merciful to you despite your sin, you should extend mercy toward those who have wronged you.

TODAY'S PLAN

Have you accepted God's mercy and extended the same kind of mercy to those who have hurt you?

SEPTEMBER

BIBLE

TODAY'S PROMISE

The grass withers and the flowers fade, but the word of our God stands forever. —ISAIAH 40:8

TODAY'S THOUGHT

Because the Bible contains the very words of the almighty God, it is the only document that is "living." In other words, it is relevant for all people in all places in all times. It is as contemporary as the latest trend yet as lasting as eternity.

TODAY'S PLAN

How is the Bible as relevant for you today as it has been for God's people in the past?

INTERCESSION

TODAY'S PROMISE

You are helping us by praying for us. Then many people will give thanks because God has graciously answered so many prayers for our safety.

—2 CORINTHIANS 1:11

TODAY'S THOUGHT

Intercession is the practice of praying for the needs of others. The Bible promises that when you pray for others, it makes a difference. Paul was convinced that the prayers of the Corinthians were vitally connected to his deliverance by God. It is easy to become discouraged if you think there is nothing anyone can do to help you—or nothing you can do to help someone you care about. But the most important thing that you and others can do is to pray. In ways beyond our understanding, intercessory prayer opens the door so that the love and power of God can pour through it into someone's life. It also causes you to care more about them. Interceding with God for others is a vital source of hope.

TODAY'S PLAN

Who might need your prayers of intercession today?

SEPTEMBER 3

PRAYER

Today's Promise

I love the LORD because he hears my voice and my prayer for mercy. Because he bends down to listen, I will pray as long as I have breath! —PSALM 116:1-2

Today's Thought

God listens carefully to and answers every prayer. His answer may be yes, no, or wait, just as loving parents might give any of these three responses to the requests of their child. Answering yes to every request would spoil you and endanger your well-being. Answering no to every request would be vindictive, stingy, and hard on your spirit. Answering wait to every request would frustrate you. God always answers your prayers according to what he knows is best for you. Knowing that God always listens and answers should inspire you to pray continually, even if his answer is not always the one you wanted.

Today's Plan

How can you begin to recognize how God is answering each of your prayers?

CHURCH

TODAY'S PROMISE

Just as our bodies have many parts and each part has a special function, so it is with Christ's body. We are many parts of one body, and we all belong to each other. In his grace, God has given us different gifts for doing certain things well. So if God has given you the ability to prophesy, speak out with as much faith as God has given you.

—ROMANS 12:4-6

TODAY'S THOUGHT

Church isn't about you and what you can get out of it. God intended the church to be a place where believers can worship him together and serve one another. If you're bored with church, it may be because you're not contributing your gifts to the body of believers or worshiping God for his sake. God promises that everyone has a special gift and thus a special role in the church. The church needs you, for the body of Christ is not complete unless you are an active part of it.

TODAY'S PLAN

How can you begin using your gifts in the church today?

MONEY

TODAY'S PROMISE

Wherever your treasure is, there the desires of your heart will also be.
—MATTHEW 6:21

TODAY'S THOUGHT

The Bible gives us many examples of wealthy people who loved God—Abraham, David, Joseph of Arimathea, Lydia. And it doesn't condemn them for their wealth. Scripture doesn't focus on how much money you have but on what you do with it. Jesus made one thing clear: Wherever your money goes, your heart will follow after it. It's fine for you to work hard and succeed without guilt. But make sure you work just as hard at finding ways to please God with your money. Otherwise your money might lead your heart away from God.

TODAY'S PLAN

Are you pleasing God by the way you spend your money?

PERFECTION

TODAY'S PROMISE

This will continue until we all come to such unity in our faith and knowledge of God's Son that we will be mature in the Lord, measuring up to the full and complete standard of Christ. —EPHESIANS 4:13

TODAY'S THOUGHT

A believer's perfection is not a flawless imitation of God but rather a process of maturing into a purer and more godly person. Growing in godliness means becoming more like God, even while falling far short of his perfect standards. That process of reflecting more and more of God's nature will be completed when you reach heaven, and then you will indeed be perfect.

TODAY'S PLAN

Where are you in the process of reaching perfection?

SEPTEMBER 7

ENEMIES

TODAY'S PROMISE

If your enemies are hungry, give them food to eat. If they are thirsty, give them water to drink. You will heap burning coals of shame on their heads, and the LORD will reward you. —PROVERBS 25:21-22

TODAY'S THOUGHT

Respond to your enemies—no matter what they do to you—with forgiveness. Your response to your enemies should include prayer as well as acts of kindness. Your words should be gentle. Your attitude should not be one of revenge or ill will. This is what Jesus would do, and when you do it too, it sets you apart from the rest of the world.

TODAY'S PLAN

What can you do today to show love to someone who is trying to hurt you?

RESPONSIBILITY

TODAY'S PROMISE

To those who use well what they are given, even more will be given, and they will have an abundance. But from those who do nothing, even what little they have will be taken away. —MATTHEW 25:29

TODAY'S THOUGHT

It seems that no one wants to take responsibility for their actions; nothing is ever "my fault." But God promises that if you take responsibility for your actions and use well what he has given you, he will give you more opportunities and more blessings. In the end, each person will be responsible for his or her own decisions, behavior, and relationships. Ultimately, everyone is responsible to God. Show responsibility in how you use the gifts and opportunities God has given you, and he will reward you.

TODAY'S PLAN

Are you taking responsibility for everything God has given you?

HIDING

TODAY'S PROMISE

From there you will search again for the LORD your God. And if you search for him with all your heart and soul, you will find him. —DEUTERONOMY 4:29

TODAY'S THOUGHT

God wants you to know him, and he reveals himself to all those who seek him. Sometimes you may try to hide from God. You blame him when you feel far away from him. You claim that God is the one playing hard to get. Perhaps you are hiding because finding God means your life will change radically. But God is always trying to show himself to you. The question is, do you really want to find him? He promises to be found when you seek him wholeheartedly.

TODAY'S PLAN

Are you hiding from God? Begin seeking him today.

REVENGE

TODAY'S PROMISE

Dear friends, never take revenge. Leave that to the righteous anger of God. For the Scriptures say, "I will take revenge; I will pay them back," says the LORD.
                                        —ROMANS 12:19

TODAY'S THOUGHT

Seeking revenge is a basic instinct of our sinful human nature. Whether we are cut off in traffic, unjustly criticized by a coworker, or the victim of a violent crime, our gut response is to get revenge. God makes it clear that vengeance is to be left to him alone. He promises to right all wrongs and get rid of evil forever on the final Day of Judgment. But for now, Jesus gives you the best example of responding to injustice with patience and kindness, and leaving judgment and punishment in the hands of God.

TODAY'S PLAN

If someone has wronged you, how can you turn your desire for revenge over to God?

ADVERSITY

TODAY'S PROMISE

God is our refuge and strength, always ready to help in times of trouble.
—PSALM 46:1

TODAY'S THOUGHT

One thing you can count on is that adversity will come. The question is, what will you do with it when it arrives? When you believe in Jesus, Satan becomes your enemy. He will try to stop you from following God by sending you all kinds of adversity. He hopes to at least make you doubt God and stop witnessing for him. Adversity may in fact be a sign that you are being faithful to God. So continue to be faithful, even when things get tough. God promises to strengthen you and help you.

TODAY'S PLAN

How can you allow adversity to draw you closer to God instead of pushing you away?

PROMISES OF GOD

TODAY'S PROMISE

God is not a man, so he does not lie. He is not human, so he does not change his mind. Has he ever spoken and failed to act? Has he ever promised and not carried it through?
                                                    —NUMBERS 23:19

TODAY'S THOUGHT

God's promises are backed by his divine character and power. If you can't believe the promises of God, you can't really believe any of God's Word. If you can't believe God's Word, then you shouldn't believe in God at all. And if you don't believe in God at all, your long-term future has no hope, for there is nothing to look forward to beyond the grave. So take comfort in the fact that you *can* believe—in his promises, in his Word, in his character, in your future, in heaven. You can believe because everything he promises comes to be.

TODAY'S PLAN

Whether or not you believe in all of God's promises determines everything else you believe or don't believe about God.

SEPTEMBER 13

CRISIS

TODAY'S PROMISE

He lifted me out of the pit of despair, out of the mud and the mire. He set my feet on solid ground and steadied me as I walked along. —PSALM 40:2

TODAY'S THOUGHT

You need not pray for the Lord to be with you in times of crisis—he already is. God promises to carry you through the crisis and give you firm footing on the other side. Then he will continue to walk with you as you wade through the aftermath.

TODAY'S PLAN

When you face a crisis, is God the first one you look to for help?

KNOWLEDGE

TODAY'S PROMISE

Fear of the LORD is the foundation of true knowledge.
—PROVERBS 1:7

TODAY'S THOUGHT

The book of Proverbs declares that the fear of the Lord is the beginning of knowledge. Our understanding of the information that the world throws at us should initially pass through the filter of God's Word. Knowledge of God and how he intended for life to work leads to purpose. When you fear God, you will spend time studying his Word and getting to know him, and you will gain true knowledge as a result.

TODAY'S PLAN

Do you look to God's Word as the source of true knowledge?

HONESTY

TODAY'S PROMISE

The LORD detests the use of dishonest scales, but he delights in accurate weights. —PROVERBS 11:1

TODAY'S THOUGHT

Honesty is essential for truth, justice, and trust in all relationships. Truth is revealed and justice carried out only when people are honest. If you can't trust your friends and family members to be honest, of if you fail to be honest with them, your relationships will crumble because of distrust and deceit. Not only will honesty safe-guard and enrich your relationships, but God delights in those who practice it.

TODAY'S PLAN

Do you need to be more honest with someone close to you?

WISDOM

TODAY'S PROMISE

If you keep yourself pure, you will be a special utensil for honorable use. Your life will be clean, and you will be ready for the Master to use you for every good work. —2 TIMOTHY 2:21

TODAY'S THOUGHT

How can you make wise decisions at a moment's notice? The key is to be prepared by developing wisdom over time. One way you do that is by keeping yourself pure—filling your mind with God's words instead of the world's advice. You can't anticipate everything that might happen today, but when you are prepared spiritually—when you have developed godly wisdom—you will know the right thing to do so God can use you to accomplish good. You will be ready to act swiftly and decisively because you have a wellspring of wisdom to draw upon.

TODAY'S PLAN

How does keeping yourself pure increase God's wisdom in your life?

BEAUTY

TODAY'S PROMISE

People judge by outward appearance, but the LORD looks at the heart. —1 SAMUEL 16:7

TODAY'S THOUGHT

Our eyes are trained to look first at someone's physical appearance. But God sees through a person's physical appearance and into the heart. Society makes us believe that an unappealing face equals an unattractive person, no matter how beautiful the person's heart is. To God, real beauty comes from who you are in your heart, not what you look like.

TODAY'S PLAN

How can you learn to see the beauty inside others instead of judging them by their outward appearance?

SECURITY

TODAY'S PROMISE

Those who fear the LORD are secure; he will be a refuge for their children. —PROVERBS 14:26

TODAY'S THOUGHT

When you strengthen your faith day by day with the truths of God's Word, you build a solid foundation that will not easily crack under pressure. When life's battles come your way, the attacks may be strong enough to knock down some of your walls, but your foundation will remain steady and secure because God's truths are eternal. You will always have a secure foundation when you trust and fear God.

TODAY'S PLAN

Where do you find security in your life?

FAITH

TODAY'S PROMISE

[Jesus said,] "I tell you the truth, if you had faith even as small as a mustard seed, you could say to this mountain, 'Move from here to there,' and it would move. Nothing would be impossible."

—MATTHEW 17:20

TODAY'S THOUGHT

The mustard seed was one of the smallest seeds people knew of, so it was often used to illustrate something of the tiniest size. Jesus says that faith is not a matter of size or quantity. It is not the size of your faith but the size of the One in whom you put your faith that makes the difference. You do not have to have great faith in God; rather, you have faith in a great God.

TODAY'S PLAN

Are you trying too hard to achieve great faith, or are you relying on a great God?

COMPROMISE

TODAY'S PROMISE

You will be successful if you carefully obey the decrees and regulations that the LORD gave to Israel through Moses. Be strong and courageous; do not be afraid or lose heart! —1 CHRONICLES 22:13

TODAY'S THOUGHT

It is never beneficial to compromise your Christian convictions. When temptations come, the only appropriate response is to resist. Sometimes you actually need to walk—or run—away. God will give you the strength and courage to obey him so that you don't compromise your faith, and he promises you will be successful as a result.

TODAY'S PLAN

What temptation do you need to resist today so you don't compromise God's ways?

RELATIONSHIPS

TODAY'S PROMISE

Hatred stirs up quarrels, but love makes up for all offenses.

—PROVERBS 10:12

TODAY'S THOUGHT

Relationships that are built on love—the kind of unconditional love God has for us—are characterized by complete and undivided devotion, forgiveness, patience, kindness, love for truth, love for justice, looking for the best in others, loyalty at any cost, and believing in the other person, no matter what. Love prohibits jealousy, envy, pride, haughtiness, selfishness, rudeness, demanding one's own way, irritability, and holding grudges. God promises that unconditionally loving others will bring healing to your relationships.

TODAY'S PLAN

Do you have any damaged relationships that could be healed by unconditional love?

OBEDIENCE

TODAY'S PROMISE

*Love the LORD your God and . . . keep his
commands, decrees, and regulations by walking
in his ways. If you do this, you will live and . . .
the LORD your God will bless you.*

—DEUTERONOMY 30:16

TODAY'S THOUGHT

Serving God with your entire life begins with
making smaller decisions to serve him in little
ways. Commit yourself to making the little, daily
choices to serve God. The more you serve him in
the little things, the more you will obey him in all
things. Obedience comes out of a lifelong commitment to making godly choices on a daily basis.

TODAY'S PLAN

What small step of obedience can you take today?

BLESSINGS

TODAY'S PROMISE

Joyful are those who have the God of Israel as their helper, whose hope is in the LORD their God.

—PSALM 146:5

TODAY'S THOUGHT

Throughout the Bible, we find a simple but profound principle: Obeying God brings blessings, but disobeying God brings misfortune. Don't think of these promised blessings only in terms of material possessions. The greatest blessings are far more valuable than money or possessions. They include joy, family, relationships, peace of heart, spiritual gifts, and the confidence of eternal life. A life focused on God brings joy and many blessings. The more you trust and obey God, the more you will experience his blessings.

TODAY'S PLAN

What are some of the greatest blessings you've experienced because of obeying God?

HUMILITY

TODAY'S PROMISE

Humble yourselves under the mighty power of God, and at the right time he will lift you up in honor.

—1 PETER 5:6

TODAY'S THOUGHT

Pride can keep you from seeking the help you need. Humility gives you the wisdom and courage to admit your needs in any situation. You won't get help—from God or from others—if you can't admit you have a problem. But when you are humble, God's power is at your disposal, and he promises to help you.

TODAY'S PLAN

Is there an area in your life where you need to be more humble?

DIVERSITY

TODAY'S PROMISE

If the ear says, "I am not part of the body because I am not an eye," would that make it any less a part of the body? If the whole body were an eye, how would you hear? . . . But our bodies have many parts, and God has put each part just where he wants it.

—1 CORINTHIANS 12:15-18

TODAY'S THOUGHT

The apostle Paul likens the church to the human body. It is foolish to try to determine whether your hand or your foot is more important—you need both. God created every believer to serve a certain role in his Kingdom, and when everyone works together, the Kingdom grows and flourishes! The more you appreciate the diversity in the body of Christ, the more you will be able to accomplish together for the glory of God.

TODAY'S PLAN

How can you accept and even celebrate the diversity you see among those you worship with?

GUIDANCE

TODAY'S PROMISE

If you need wisdom, ask our generous God, and he will give it to you. He will not rebuke you for asking.

—JAMES 1:5

TODAY'S THOUGHT

Have you ever asked God for a sign? Sometimes we want to ask God to perform a miracle so that his guidance will be crystal clear. Although God sometimes works that way, most often he does not. The best place to find God's guidance is in his Word, the Bible. If you want God to personally guide you, study the Bible. He intended it as a guidebook for getting through life. God also wants you to have faith, to trust him every step of the way. So read the Bible, ask God what to do next, and then take a step of faith every day. God promises he will lead you in the right direction.

TODAY'S PLAN

As you read God's Word today, what do you think God is guiding you to do?

CHANGE

TODAY'S PROMISE

Anyone who belongs to Christ has become a new person. The old life is gone; a new life has begun!

—2 CORINTHIANS 5:17

TODAY'S THOUGHT

Change is one of the constants of life. The Bible teaches two great truths about change. The first is that despite the changing world around us, God is changeless and dependable. The second is that God requires an inner change of heart, called repentance, that produces an outward change of lifestyle, called obedience. When your heart is changed, your life will be changed forever.

TODAY'S PLAN

Have the unchanging truths of Scripture changed your heart and life?

HAPPINESS

TODAY'S PROMISE

How joyful are those who fear the LORD and delight in obeying his commands. —PSALM 112:1

TODAY'S THOUGHT

Happiness is a fleeting emotion that is based on your circumstances. God does not promise that your life will always be happy. But God does promise a joy that goes deeper than happiness for all those who sincerely follow him. If you trust him, you have the assurance that the God of the universe loves you, wants to know you, promises to comfort and care for you, and has guaranteed your eternal future with him. This kind of joy stays with you even when happiness is unattainable.

TODAY'S PLAN

Is your life characterized more by happiness or joy?

OPPRESSION

TODAY'S PROMISE

The Spirit of the LORD is upon me, for he has anointed me to bring Good News to the poor. He has sent me to proclaim that captives will be released, that the blind will see, that the oppressed will be set free, and that the time of the LORD's favor has come.

—LUKE 4:18-19

TODAY'S THOUGHT

Jesus came to deliver people who are oppressed by the world and the powers of evil. We see this throughout the Gospels. He delivered people from spiritual oppression by driving out demons. He delivered them from physical oppression by healing their diseases. He delivered them from intellectual oppression by exposing lies and teaching the truth that would set them free. And he spoke boldly against oppressive spiritual leadership. Jesus promises to deliver you not only from the consequences of your sins but from all the forces that oppress you in this world.

TODAY'S PLAN

How are you oppressed by the world or the devil? Have you asked Jesus to set you free?

EVIL

TODAY'S PROMISE

Though the wicked sprout like weeds and evildoers flourish, they will be destroyed forever. —PSALM 92:7

TODAY'S THOUGHT

Sometimes it seems as if evil people can do anything they want—and not only do they get away with it, they flourish. God has promised, however, that in his time, everyone will be judged, evil will be exposed, and the righteous will prevail. God doesn't promise the absence of evil on this earth. In fact, he warns that evil will be pervasive and powerful. But God promises to help you stand against evil. When you do, you will receive your reward of eternal life with him in heaven, where evil will be banished forever.

TODAY'S PLAN

Stop asking why some people get away with evil and start asking God to give you the strength to combat evil when you come face-to-face with it.

OCTOBER

CARE

TODAY'S PROMISE

Give all your worries and cares to God, for he cares about you. —1 PETER 5:7

TODAY'S THOUGHT

How does God care for you? Can you count the ways? God is always close to you, ready to help in your time of need. God's presence surrounds you, protecting you from Satan's attacks. God sends you opportunities to make your life more full and satisfying. He sends you countless blessings. He promises to take your worries and cares upon himself. And he offers you eternal life in heaven, away from all hurt, pain, and sin.

TODAY'S PLAN

How can you give to God your worries and cares today and focus instead on how he cares for you?

NEEDS

TODAY'S PROMISE

God blesses those who are poor and realize their need for him, for the Kingdom of Heaven is theirs.

—MATTHEW 5:3

TODAY'S THOUGHT

All people have basic needs that must be met in order to survive, including food, water, shelter, and love. When your needs are met, you can be content and satisfied. Wants, even when fulfilled, often leave you unsatisfied, discontent, and desiring more. Wants are not always negative, but sometimes they are contrary to what God desires for you. Wants can lead you into sin if you become obsessed with pursuing them. Having your needs met often allows God to show his power and provision through you and to teach you that he is sufficient. Learning the difference between your needs and your wants allows you to find contentment in God's sustaining power and provision.

TODAY'S PLAN

How often do you acknowledge that your greatest need is for God?

CIRCUMSTANCES

TODAY'S PROMISE

Blessed are those who trust in the LORD and have made the LORD their hope and confidence. They are like trees planted along a riverbank, with roots that reach deep into the water. Such trees are not bothered by the heat or worried by long months of drought. Their leaves stay green, and they never stop producing fruit. —JEREMIAH 17:7-8

TODAY'S THOUGHT

God uses your circumstances, good or bad, to help you—and others—to grow. It's easy to be joyful and faithful when life is going well, but when life gets tough, believers have a unique opportunity to show how a relationship with God brings comfort, confidence, and hope. When you glorify God in the most difficult of circumstances, two wonderful things happen: You learn to rely on God instead of yourself, and others are blessed by seeing your faith and hope in action.

TODAY'S PLAN

In what ways do you rely on God's help when bad circumstances come along?

OPPOSITION

TODAY'S PROMISE

If the world hates you, remember that it hated me first. . . . I chose you to come out of the world, so it hates you.
—JOHN 15:18-19

If God is for us, who can ever be against us?
—ROMANS 8:31

TODAY'S THOUGHT

Evil can't stand the sight of Jesus, can't bear even to hear his name. If you are living so that others can clearly see Jesus in you, there is good news and bad news. The bad news is that you will face opposition and even persecution for your faith. Satan opposes Jesus, so if you are on Jesus' side, Satan is your enemy too. The good news is that even if the whole world is against you, God is for you. He promises to give you spiritual victories in this life and ultimate victory in heaven for eternity.

TODAY'S PLAN

In what areas of your life do you feel spiritual opposition?

FORGIVENESS

TODAY'S PROMISE

Though your sins are like scarlet, I will make them as white as snow. Though they are red like crimson, I will make them as white as wool. —ISAIAH 1:18

TODAY'S THOUGHT

Forgiveness means that God looks at you as though you have never sinned. It means you become blameless before him. When God forgives you, he doesn't just sweep your sins under the carpet. Instead, he completely washes them away and makes you as pure and perfect as his Son, Jesus.

TODAY'S PLAN

Have you asked for God's forgiveness and experienced the complete removal of your past sins?

OCTOBER 6

DEPENDENCE

TODAY'S PROMISE

Those who trust in idols, who say, "You are our gods," will be turned away in shame. —ISAIAH 42:17

TODAY'S THOUGHT

An idol is anything that takes God's place in your heart. Money, convenience, hobbies, reputation, beauty, celebrities, success—any of these can be idols if they become more important to you than God. When you stop depending on God, you begin to separate yourself from him. You start to go your own way and neglect his Word and his ways. Neglect leads to disobedience and sin, and God may choose to discipline you in order to lead you back to him. You can't experience God's best for you if you depend on anyone or anything besides him.

TODAY'S PLAN

Are there idols in your life that you have become dependent on?

HEALING

TODAY'S PROMISE

For you who fear my name, the Sun of Righteousness will rise with healing in his wings. And you will go free, leaping with joy like calves let out to pasture.

—MALACHI 4:2

TODAY'S THOUGHT

He who created your body, mind, and soul can certainly repair and restore them. A relationship with God is a powerful source of healing because it connects you with your Creator. God loves you so much that he allowed his Son to suffer and die in your place. He promises that in eternity you will be fully healed.

TODAY'S PLAN

What kind of healing are you looking forward to today?

CONFIDENCE

TODAY'S PROMISE

Those who are righteous will be long remembered. They do not fear bad news; they confidently trust the LORD to care for them. They are confident and fearless and can face their foes triumphantly.

—PSALM 112:6-8

TODAY'S THOUGHT

Confidence depends on complete consistency between words and actions, projections and outcomes. You can be completely confident in what God's Word says because God has never broken a single promise. He has always done what he said he would, and he will always do what he says he will.

TODAY'S PLAN

How can you increase your confidence in God and his promises?

FOLLOWING

TODAY'S PROMISE

[Jesus said,] "My sheep listen to my voice; I know them, and they follow me." —JOHN 10:27

TODAY'S THOUGHT

Being a disciple of Jesus is simply a matter of following him with a willing heart. To follow him, you must learn to hear and recognize his voice. You can do this by studying his Word, the Bible. He will bless you not because of your ability but because of your availability.

TODAY'S PLAN

How much do you really want to follow Jesus?

APPROVAL

TODAY'S PROMISE

The Kingdom of God is not a matter of what we eat or drink, but of living a life of goodness and peace and joy in the Holy Spirit. If you serve Christ with this attitude, you will please God, and others will approve of you, too.
—ROMANS 14:17-18

TODAY'S THOUGHT

Seek God's approval first. Sometimes doing what pleases God also pleases others, especially godly people, but that is not always the case. God has many enemies who love evil more than good, so you may never earn their approval. Your ultimate purpose is to please the God who made you and redeemed you, no matter what others may think of you. Focus on him; he promises you will receive his approval.

TODAY'S PLAN

What might you need to change in your life today as you seek God's approval?

PURSUIT BY GOD

TODAY'S PROMISE

Long ago the LORD said . . . : "I have loved you, my people, with an everlasting love. With unfailing love I have drawn you to myself." —JEREMIAH 31:3

TODAY'S THOUGHT

God created you, loves you, and longs to have a relationship with you. So he pursues you with persistent and unfailing love. Has he caught your attention yet?

TODAY'S PLAN

How does it make you feel that God himself is pursuing you with his love?

HUMILITY

Today's Promise

All of you, serve each other in humility, for "God opposes the proud but favors the humble." —1 PETER 5:5

Today's Thought

Humility is a prerequisite for service. True humility results from understanding who you are and who God is. Humility allows you to serve wherever God places you and do whatever God asks of you. When you are sick or injured and must rely on a physician's care, you are humbled because you realize your vulnerability. Likewise, you are humbled when you realize you are completely dependent on God to heal your soul. When you have this kind of humility, you will be happy to serve your Lord in any way he asks.

Today's Plan

Do you have the humility to serve God wherever he is calling you?

ENDURANCE

TODAY'S PROMISE

*Of course, you get no credit for being patient if you
are beaten for doing wrong. But if you suffer for
doing good and endure it patiently, God is pleased
with you.*
—1 PETER 2:20

TODAY'S THOUGHT

Almost every Christian is persecuted in some
way at some point along life's journey. In many
countries, Christians suffer torture and death
for their faith. When you feel like quitting,
you are focusing too much on this life and not
enough on the life you will have for eternity if you
endure. Not only is endurance through suffering
and ridicule necessary to receive the prize of eternal life, but those who endure have a special
place in God's heart.

TODAY'S PLAN

*When you feel like quitting your walk of faith, what
motivates you to endure?*

POWER OF GOD

TODAY'S PROMISE

*It is not by force nor by strength, but by my Spirit,
says the LORD of Heaven's Armies.* —ZECHARIAH 4:6

TODAY'S THOUGHT

The Holy Spirit is the power of God that lives
in every believer. When you yield control of
your life to him, he releases his power within
you—power to resist temptation, to serve and
love God and others, to have wisdom in all circumstances, and to persevere in living for God
here with the promise of eternal life in heaven.
Through his Spirit, God will give you the power
you need to do everything he asks you to do.

TODAY'S PLAN

How can you tap into God's power?

CHALLENGES

TODAY'S PROMISE

Be strong and courageous, and do the work. Don't be afraid or discouraged, for the LORD God, my God, is with you. He will not fail you or forsake you. He will see to it that all the work . . . is finished correctly. —1 CHRONICLES 28:20

TODAY'S THOUGHT

Regardless of the size of the challenge, you have God working in you. That is sufficient to help you finish and finish well any work you have before you. God doesn't call you to a task without helping you see it through to completion. He promises to provide everything you need.

TODAY'S PLAN

If you're facing a particular challenge, how does it help to know that God is working to help you accomplish your task?

OCTOBER 16

REGRETS

Today's Promise

He saved us, not because of the righteous things we had done, but because of his mercy. He washed away our sins, giving us a new birth and new life through the Holy Spirit.

—TITUS 3:5

Today's Thought

Regrets are like a dirty window that keeps you from seeing clearly what is in front of you. But God is in the cleaning business. He washes away the sins of your past as well as the guilt you still feel over those sins. If God can completely forget your sins, so can you. You can choose to move forward joyfully and leave behind the burden of regret.

Today's Plan

Are you still carrying regrets over past sins? Ask God to wash away your guilt so you can move on in peace and joy.

GUIDANCE

TODAY'S PROMISE

You guide me with your counsel, leading me to a glorious destiny.
—PSALM 73:24

TODAY'S THOUGHT

When you travel to a new destination, you might seek the advice of someone who has been there, who knows the lay of the land, the best sites to see, and the places to avoid. As you journey through life, it is important to have a close relationship with the ultimate travel guide, Jesus Christ. He knows where you've been and what will happen in the future. When you seek his advice, he points you toward places of beauty, joy, and peace, and he helps you avoid the dangerous spots. God promises to be your constant guide on your life's journey, leading you through the dark valleys and up to the mountaintop experiences, finally bringing you to that place of eternal peace and rest you long for.

TODAY'S PLAN

When others look at the path of your life, do they see that God is guiding you?

ASSURANCE

TODAY'S PROMISE

This High Priest of ours understands our weaknesses, for he faced all of the same testing we do, yet he did not sin. So let us come boldly to the throne of our gracious God. There we will receive his mercy, and we will find grace to help us when we need it most.   —HEBREWS 4:15-16

TODAY'S THOUGHT

Don't ever be afraid to talk to God. When you get to know him, you'll discover that he's not a harsh dictator, ready to punish you for every fault. He's a loving father, wanting to comfort, help, forgive, and bless you. The assurance of God's love gives you courage to come to him with any problem, struggle, or concern. He will always open the door so you can talk with him as long as you want.

TODAY'S PLAN

How can the assurance of God's love help you talk more openly with him?

HOLINESS

TODAY'S PROMISE

Our High Priest offered himself to God as a single sacrifice for sins, good for all time. Then he sat down in the place of honor at God's right hand. . . . For by that one offering he forever made perfect those who are being made holy. —HEBREWS 10:12-14

TODAY'S THOUGHT

On your own, it is not possible to be holy because you were born with a bent toward sin. But when you ask God's Holy Spirit to control your mind and actions, you take the first important step toward becoming more holy. Holiness here on earth does not equal perfection; it means striving for purity. But God promises that you will one day be perfectly holy in heaven.

TODAY'S PLAN

How can you strive to be holy today?

JUDGMENT

TODAY'S PROMISE

The Lord is coming with countless thousands of his holy ones to execute judgment on the people of the world. He will convict every person of all the ungodly things they have done and for all the insults that ungodly sinners have spoken against him.

—JUDE 1:14–15

TODAY'S THOUGHT

Anyone who has not followed Jesus Christ as Lord will be judged on the last day and sentenced to eternity in hell. You can argue that it's not fair, that no "good" person should go to hell. But God gives an open invitation to everyone. Many people will be dismayed on Judgment Day to find that living a good life and being successful are not enough. God displays his justice when he honors the choice someone has made to follow him or not.

TODAY'S PLAN

Is eternity in hell worth rejecting God's plan of salvation?

BALANCE

TODAY'S PROMISE

Letting your sinful nature control your mind leads to death. But letting the Spirit control your mind leads to life and peace. —ROMANS 8:6

TODAY'S THOUGHT

It's a mistake to allow your life to get out of balance by overemphasizing one of your responsibilities at the cost of others. Balance means using your gifts, time, and resources to live a life that honors God. It means caring for others and yourself. God assures you there is time for everything he calls you to do. Jesus, despite his power and the needs of those around him, left much undone; yet he completed everything God had planned for him to do. When you try to accomplish everything you want to get done, you usually feel unsatisfied. But when you let the Holy Spirit control your life, the balance he brings gives you peace of heart and mind.

TODAY'S PLAN

Do you feel out of control? As you give more control of your life to the Holy Spirit, you will find balance.

HONESTY

TODAY'S PROMISE

The Scriptures say, "If you want to enjoy life and see many happy days, keep your tongue from speaking evil and your lips from telling lies." —1 PETER 3:10

TODAY'S THOUGHT

Lying is deceiving someone. It can be blatant or subtle. Lying is selfish and self-serving, for it always attempts to hide and deceive, to take what you have not earned, or to leave an impression you do not deserve. To fall short of truth, in any way, is to lie. You cannot follow the God of truth while you consistently tell lies—even "little white lies." Lying destroys trust, and trust is the key to strong relationships. That is why the Bible promises that a happy life is an honest life.

TODAY'S PLAN

How can you be completely honest today and feel happier as a result?

BROKENNESS

TODAY'S PROMISE

The sacrifice you desire is a broken spirit. You will not reject a broken and repentant heart, O God.

—PSALM 51:17

TODAY'S THOUGHT

God promises to draw close to you when you are brokenhearted over sin in your life. When you repent, you turn to God in brokenness over your sin. Then he begins to heal and restore you.

TODAY'S PLAN

How often do you come to God with an attitude of brokenness over the sin in your life?

HOPE

TODAY'S PROMISE

All glory to God, who is able, through his mighty power at work within us, to accomplish infinitely more than we might ask or think. —EPHESIANS 3:20

TODAY'S THOUGHT

Most people hope too little in God and expect too little from him. If you remind yourself of the amazing things God has already done, you will have reason to believe that the sovereign Lord of the universe wants to bless you more abundantly than you can imagine.

TODAY'S PLAN

What do you dare to hope for? Have the courage to talk to God about it.

HELP

TODAY'S PROMISE

Whenever they were in trouble and turned to the LORD, the God of Israel, and sought him out, they found him.
                                                      —2 CHRONICLES 15:4

TODAY'S THOUGHT

God helps you by always being available. He is ready and willing to help you whenever you call out to him. Prayer is the lifeline that connects you to God. Use it daily, and receive the help you need.

TODAY'S PLAN

Have you asked God for help yet today?

PEACE

TODAY'S PROMISE

Wherever there is jealousy and selfish ambition, there you will find disorder and evil of every kind. . . . Those who are peacemakers will plant seeds of peace and reap a harvest of righteousness. —JAMES 3:16-18

TODAY'S THOUGHT

Peace and security come when you live in harmony with God's commands. Two of God's most important commands are to love him and to love others. When everyone makes their own rules instead of following God's standards, chaos reigns. When people put their own desires above the needs of others, chaos and confusion rule their lives. But when God's commands rule your life, order and purpose come into your life. You grow in wisdom and find peace for your mind and heart.

TODAY'S PLAN

If your life is chaotic, what can you do to experience peace and order today?

LOVE OF GOD

TODAY'S PROMISE

The LORD says, "I will rescue those who love me. I will protect those who trust in my name. When they call on me, I will answer; I will be with them in trouble. I will rescue and honor them. I will reward them with a long life and give them my salvation."
—PSALM 91:14-16

TODAY'S THOUGHT

God loves you because he made you. You are not a creature that randomly evolved from a prehistoric primordial soup. God created you in his own image so you could have a relationship with him. God desires your love and friendship, and he is pursuing you now. Stop running from him, and discover the purpose for which he made you.

TODAY'S PLAN

Have you realized that God is pursuing you with his love, or are you running from him?

GREED

TODAY'S PROMISE

Give freely and become more wealthy; be stingy and lose everything. —PROVERBS 11:24

TODAY'S THOUGHT

The more obsessed you are with getting more, the greater the odds that you will wind up with less. Greed is dangerous because left unchecked it can become so powerful that it will control your life. More is never enough when you are seeking things that can't truly satisfy. Generosity is the opposite of greed. God promises that the more you give, the more you will receive.

TODAY'S PLAN

How tightly do you hold on to what you have?

COPING

TODAY'S PROMISE

The LORD helps the fallen and lifts those bent beneath their loads. —PSALM 145:14

TODAY'S THOUGHT

Life is stressful. Every day, new challenges and pressures come your way. Hard times are inevitable. Sometimes you wonder how you can cope with it all. You can't control your circumstances, but you can control how you respond to them and whom you go to for help. You need the proper perspective to cope with life. God encourages you not to run away from your problems or try to escape them but to work through them. Then you will come out stronger on the other side. Through it all, God offers strength and wisdom that you cannot find anywhere else. How you respond to the challenges of life, including how much you rely on God, determines how well you cope.

TODAY'S PLAN

Are you coping with life from God's perspective?

PERSEVERANCE

TODAY'S PROMISE

All the while, you will grow as you learn to know God better and better. We also pray that you will be strengthened with all his glorious power so you will have all the endurance and patience you need.

—COLOSSIANS 1:10-11

TODAY'S THOUGHT

The fuel you need to persevere through life is the power of God working in you. As you become more obedient and more in tune with God, God's power will strengthen you and ignite your ability to persevere—not just to endure, but to persevere with joy!

TODAY'S PLAN

What can you do to develop more perseverance?

PURITY

TODAY'S PROMISE

Teach me your ways, O LORD, that I may live according to your truth! Grant me purity of heart, so that I may honor you.

—PSALM 86:11

TODAY'S THOUGHT

One bad apple spoils the barrel. Likewise, just a little bit of sin in our lives spoils our relationship with God and with others and causes us to become spiritually sick. But Jesus' death on the cross purified our contaminated lives so that we could be fresh and clean in the presence of God. We cannot accomplish this on our own. God's forgiveness is like an ever-blooming tree of perfect fruit in our lives. When you humbly ask him to forgive you, he removes the contamination of your sin and makes you fresh and pure again.

TODAY'S PLAN

How much has sin spoiled your life? How can you become pure?

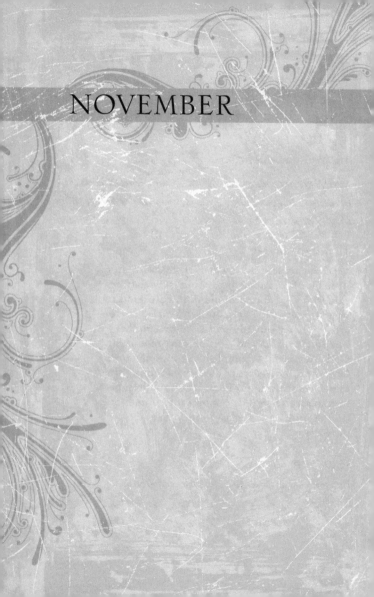

NOVEMBER

SATISFACTION

TODAY'S PROMISE

Just as Death and Destruction are never satisfied, so human desire is never satisfied. —PROVERBS 27:20

TODAY'S THOUGHT

Just as drinking saltwater actually makes you thirstier, the Bible promises that getting more of something actually makes you less satisfied. When you get what you want, you will still want more of it. The perpetual quest to satisfy your desires leaves a growing, consuming emptiness that is never filled. The desire to be satisfied with earthly things (money, achievements) perpetuates a cycle of dissatisfaction, a never-ending drive for just one more thing. As a result, you are never satisfied with what you have. The sooner you understand this principle, the sooner you can begin to find true satisfaction by letting go of the temporary and seeking after the eternal.

TODAY'S PLAN

Are you becoming less satisfied with what life has to offer? What does God offer that truly satisfies?

NOVEMBER 2

INTEGRITY

TODAY'S PROMISE

Who may worship in your sanctuary, LORD? . . .
Those who lead blameless lives and do what is right,
speaking the truth from sincere hearts. Those who
refuse to gossip or harm their neighbors or speak evil
of their friends. Those who . . . keep their promises
even when it hurts. Those who . . . cannot be
bribed to lie about the innocent. Such people
will stand firm forever.
—PSALM 15:1-5

TODAY'S THOUGHT

Integrity means living a life that is consistent in
belief and behavior, in words and deeds. Your
integrity is reflected in your relationship with
God and with other people. Live an honest
life in all your dealings with people—even
when it doesn't seem to benefit you. Those
who commit themselves to a life of integrity
have a firm foundation that will last into
eternity.

TODAY'S PLAN

What one thing can you do today to live with integrity?

CONTENTMENT

TODAY'S PROMISE

Don't love money; be satisfied with what you have. For God has said, "I will never fail you. I will never abandon you." —HEBREWS 13:5

After all, we brought nothing with us when we came into the world, and we can't take anything with us when we leave it. —1 TIMOTHY 6:7

TODAY'S THOUGHT

Contentment comes when you have a proper perspective of eternity. It's not how much you accumulate on earth but how much you send on to heaven. The heart and soul that make you who you are follow you into eternity; the money and things that make up what you have stay here.

TODAY'S PLAN

How might a heavenly perspective affect your current level of contentment?

MISTAKES

TODAY'S PROMISE

He has removed our sins as far from us as the east is from the west.

—PSALM 103:12

TODAY'S THOUGHT

There can be a difference between making a mistake and committing a sin. For example, accidentally saying something hurtful is a mistake. Gossiping or slandering someone is a sin. You can often avoid repeating a mistake by studying where you went wrong in the past, planning better, and double-checking your words and actions. But to avoid repeating a sin, you need God's help. The regret you feel over a sin indicates that you want to change your ways. When you confess your sin to God, he promises to change you by removing your sin and your regret.

TODAY'S PLAN

Have you asked God to help you avoid both careless mistakes and outright sin?

ADVICE

TODAY'S PROMISE

Anyone who wanders away from this teaching has no relationship with God. But anyone who remains in the teaching of Christ has a relationship with both the Father and the Son. —2 JOHN 1:9

TODAY'S THOUGHT

One way to evaluate advice is to evaluate the advisers. Do their actions match their words? The most important way to evaluate advice is to check it against the truth of God's Word. If it contradicts the Bible, then it is bad advice. Don't make a habit of following bad advice, or eventually you will not be able to tell the difference between good and bad advice, causing you to lose touch with God. Listen to God's advice, and you will always stay close to him.

TODAY'S PLAN

How do you evaluate the advice you receive?

MONEY

TODAY'S PROMISE

Teach those who are rich in this world not to be proud and not to trust in their money, which is so unreliable. Their trust should be in God, who richly gives us all we need for our enjoyment. . . . They should be rich in good works and generous to those in need. By doing this they will be storing up their treasure as a good foundation for the future so that they may experience true life.

—1 TIMOTHY 6:17-1

TODAY'S THOUGHT

We are accountable for how we use the money God has entrusted to us, so use it to honor Go and help others. Learn and share with other God's principles about earning money, giving generously, saving regularly, and spending responsibly. Understand the link between how you use your money on earth and the corresponding rewards in heaven.

TODAY'S PLAN

How can you invest wealth in heaven by spending you money here on earth more wisely?

DIFFERENCES

TODAY'S PROMISE

Live in harmony and peace. Then the God of love and peace will be with you. —2 CORINTHIANS 13:11

TODAY'S THOUGHT

One of our greatest challenges is remembering why God made us different and then focusing on how those differences can help us work together. We must not allow our differences to set us against each other. Instead, our differences should bring us together to accomplish more than we ever thought possible. When you and other Christians use your differences in harmony, God promises to live among you and bless you with peace.

TODAY'S PLAN

Do you know someone who is so different from you that you can't seem to get along? How might those differences help bring you together, with God's help?

BELONGING

TODAY'S PROMISE

Now you are no longer a slave but God's own child. And since you are his child, God has made you his heir.

—GALATIANS 4:

TODAY'S THOUGHT

Belonging to God means you are no longer a slave to whatever your sinful nature tempts you to do. Therefore, you are no longer guilty before God. Now you are forgiven and free to receive all the blessings he graciously gives to his children. You will inherit the privileges of belonging to the family of God.

TODAY'S PLAN

What privileges does God promise you because you belong to him?

GRIEF

TODAY'S PROMISE

I will be glad and rejoice in your unfailing love, for you have seen my troubles, and you care about the anguish of my soul.
—PSALM 31:7

TODAY'S THOUGHT

Grief brings suffering, anxiety, confusion, rest-lessness, pain, heartache, and usually plenty of tears. Some grief, like that of losing a loved one, can be understood only by those who have walked its dark valley before you. Grief is like a stabbing pain. It tortures your soul and robs you of the joy of living. But you can find this theme throughout the Bible: Even when you go through dark times of grief, God is with you, blessing you with comfort and hope. Not only that, God also promises that one day he will turn your sorrow into joy.

TODAY'S PLAN

When you are grieving, which of God's promises comfort you most?

INJUSTICE

TODAY'S PROMISE

Fear the LORD and judge with integrity, for the LORD our God does not tolerate perverted justice, partiality, or the taking of bribes. —2 CHRONICLES 19:

TODAY'S THOUGHT

God allows injustice for the present time, but he will not tolerate it forever. Injustice happens because of sin in the world and the sinful nature of human beings. The existence of injustice does not mean that God condones it. That is contrary to his nature and opposed to what the Bible teaches. God sees every injustice and judges it to be sin. He promises to bring an end to all injustice at the final judgment.

TODAY'S PLAN

How can you be just in all your thoughts and actions today?

FREEDOM

TODAY'S PROMISE

We give great honor to those who endure under suffering.
—JAMES 5:11

TODAY'S THOUGHT

Every country honors its soldiers who endure much suffering on behalf of its citizens. Soldiers are heroes who are willing to give up their lives so that others can live life to the fullest. The Christian faith also has heroes—those who inspire us to hang on to our faith no matter what happens, those who are willing to give up their lives for what they believe. When you are faithful to God no matter what, you will experience the greatest of freedoms—freedom from sin and eternal death.

TODAY'S PLAN

You may never face martyrdom for being a Christian, but is your faith strong enough to endure even a little suffering?

NOVEMBER 12

THANKFULNESS

TODAY'S PROMISE

Giving thanks is a sacrifice that truly honors me. If you keep to my path, I will reveal to you the salvation of God.

—PSALM 50:23

TODAY'S THOUGHT

The Bible says that thanking God is a sacrifice that honors him. A thankful heart honors God for what he has done and recognizes his work, mercy, provision, and blessing in your life. A thankful heart gives you a positive attitude because it keeps you focused on everything God is doing for you instead of what you think you lack. Give thanks to God every day—he promises to bless you with his salvation.

TODAY'S PLAN

What can you thank God for today?

COMFORT

TODAY'S PROMISE

All praise to God, the Father of our Lord Jesus Christ. God is our merciful Father and the source of all comfort. He comforts us in all our troubles so that we can comfort others. When they are troubled, we will be able to give them the same comfort God has given us. —2 CORINTHIANS 1:3-4

TODAY'S THOUGHT

Remember the ways that God has comforted you in times of trouble, and model that kind of comfort to others. When you have experienced God's assuring love, his guiding wisdom, and his sustaining power, you understand what others need and are better able to comfort them. The comforted become the comforters.

TODAY'S PLAN

Do you know someone who needs your comfort today?

GRIEF

TODAY'S PROMISE

You keep track of all my sorrows. You have collected all my tears in your bottle. You have recorded each one in your book. —PSALM 56:8

TODAY'S THOUGHT

Even people who have a relationship with God through Jesus Christ grieve during times of loss. But Christians can grieve with hope. You grieve because you experience the real pain of the loss, but you can grieve with hope because you know that God notices your sorrow and will redeem your tragedy. God does not waste your sorrows but brings something good out of them if you let him do his transforming work in you.

TODAY'S PLAN

Even in the midst of sorrow, are you able to grieve with hope?

JUDGMENT

TODAY'S PROMISE

Since we have been made right in God's sight by the blood of Christ, he will certainly save us from God's condemnation. For since our friendship with God was restored by the death of his Son while we were still his enemies, we will certainly be saved through the life of his Son. —ROMANS 5:9-10

TODAY'S THOUGHT

Because we like to be in control, one of the hardest things to accept is that we don't make the rules for how life and faith work—God does. God's rules say that sin deserves eternal death, and everyone has sinned. Your assurance for salvation is based on the fact that Jesus Christ stood in your place and took the judgment you deserved for your sin. God promises that he no longer judges you an enemy but a friend—even his own child.

TODAY'S PLAN

How will you be able to face the judgment of God?

CHARACTER

TODAY'S PROMISE

Make every effort to respond to God's promises. . . . The more you grow like this, the more productive and useful you will be in your knowledge of our Lord Jesus Christ.

—2 PETER 1:5, 8

TODAY'S THOUGHT

As you mature in your faith, you will develop inner strength of character, giving you spiritual wisdom and power that can help you accomplish more than you ever thought possible. As your confidence in God's promises increases, so does your knowledge of Jesus and the assurance of God's love for you. These are the building blocks of an unshakable character.

TODAY'S PLAN

How can a strong character help you be more productive and useful for God?

FEAR

TODAY'S PROMISE

I am leaving you with a gift—peace of mind and heart. And the peace I give is a gift the world cannot give. So don't be troubled or afraid.

—JOHN 14:27

TODAY'S THOUGHT

When you feel afraid, remember that no enemy, no adversity, can take away your most important blessings—your relationship with God, his forgiveness of your sins, and your eternal salvation. These remain secure even when your world falls apart. Your situation may be genuinely threatening, but God has not abandoned you. He promises to stay with you. Even if your troubles should end in death, God has not left you. He has instead ushered you into his very presence.

TODAY'S PLAN

What are you afraid of today? How can you remember that God is still with you?

BLESSINGS

TODAY'S PROMISE

Blessed are those who trust in the LORD and have made the LORD their hope and confidence.

—JEREMIAH 17:7

TODAY'S THOUGHT

What does it mean to be blessed by God? Receiving God's blessing means not only enjoying many gifts—such as life, joy, peace, abundance, children, home, reputation, health, freedom, work, food—but being welcomed into a special relationship with him, which carries rich meaning and satisfaction. When you experience this special relationship with God, you understand that all you are and all you have are blessings from him that can in turn be used to bless others.

TODAY'S PLAN

Are you fully experiencing God's blessings?

DECISIONS

TODAY'S PROMISE

Who are those who fear the LORD? He will show them the path they should choose. —PSALM 25:12

TODAY'S THOUGHT

The Bible says that if you "fear the Lord," he will guide you through life. To fear the Lord means to respect him enough to obey him. When you decide to obey him, you will follow him. And when you follow him, he will lead you to places and opportunities where you can best serve him and others. If you want to make good decisions, first decide to obey God. Then you know you will be going in the right direction with your other decisions.

TODAY'S PLAN

How can obedience to God lead you to make better decisions?

KINDNESS

TODAY'S PROMISE

The LORD is merciful and compassionate, slow to get angry and filled with unfailing love. . . . The LORD is righteous in everything he does; he is filled with kindness.

—PSALM 145:8, 17

TODAY'S THOUGHT

God promises to give you mercy when you don't deserve it, to be patient and not lash out in anger when you do something wrong. In other words, he promises to love you unconditionally, even if you don't return his love. God didn't just create kindness, he *is* kindness. Everything he does for you is an act of kindness. He wants you to become everything he created you to be and give you every opportunity to experience the joy of eternity with him.

TODAY'S PLAN

How can you be aware of God's kindness toward you today?

GIVING

TODAY'S PROMISE

You must each decide in your heart how much to give. And don't give reluctantly or in response to pressure. "For God loves a person who gives cheerfully." —2 CORINTHIANS 9:7

TODAY'S THOUGHT

Giving gifts to God glorifies him. It enriches your life and the lives of others. You will experience God's generosity and be fulfilled by God's blessings. Those who benefit from your gifts will thank God and honor him as their needs are met, and they will be encouraged to continue the cycle of giving.

TODAY'S PLAN

What gift can you give someone today that would initiate a cycle of giving?

GRACE

TODAY'S PROMISE

The LORD is compassionate and merciful, slow to get angry and filled with unfailing love. —PSALM 103:8

TODAY'S THOUGHT

Your beliefs about God are more important than any other beliefs you have. If you believe that God is always angry with you, you will likely be defensive, fearful, or antagonistic toward him. But when you believe that God shows you deep love and grace, you can live in the joy of being forgiven and knowing you will live forever in heaven with him. You will no longer fear God's retribution but will thank him for his grace.

TODAY'S PLAN

Do you believe in a God who is full of anger or a God who is full of grace?

HEAVEN

TODAY'S PROMISE

Let me reveal to you a wonderful secret. We will not all die, but we will all be transformed! It will happen in a moment, in the blink of an eye, when the last trumpet is blown. For when the trumpet sounds, those who have died will be raised to live forever. And we who are living will also be transformed. For our dying bodies must be transformed into bodies that will never die; our mortal bodies must be transformed into immortal bodies.

—1 CORINTHIANS 15:51-53

TODAY'S THOUGHT

One day you will be like Jesus. You will not be equal to him in power and authority, but you will be like him in character and perfection, for there will be no sin in heaven. You will never again experience pain or sorrow, and evil will be gone forever.

TODAY'S PLAN

How does your hope of heaven help you live better today?

THANKFULNESS

TODAY'S PROMISE

Give thanks for everything to God the Father in the name of our Lord Jesus Christ. —EPHESIANS 5:20

TODAY'S THOUGHT

When you give thanks to God, you honor and praise him for everything he has done—in your life, in the lives of others, in the church, in the world. Similarly, when you thank other people, you honor them and show them respect for who they are and what they have done. This attitude of gratitude helps you serve others and allows you to enjoy whatever blessings come your way.

TODAY'S PLAN

Can you commit to thanking God for something every day?

THANKFULNESS

TODAY'S PROMISE

Be thankful in all circumstances, for this is God's will for you who belong to Christ Jesus.

—1 THESSALONIANS 5:18

TODAY'S THOUGHT

Your loving spouse works hard all day, either at work or at home. Do you bother to say thanks? Think about how often in a day other people do things for you, however small. Do you remember to thank them? Now think about how often God helps you in your daily life. Think about how much God has given you. When you pause to think about it, you will see that God is continually blessing you, providing for you, and protecting you. How often do you say thanks to him? Giving thanks is a way to celebrate both the giver and the gift. Remember to thank God in everything.

TODAY'S PLAN

How often do you thank God for the blessings in your life?

DOUBT

TODAY'S PROMISE

Because of his glory and excellence, he has given us great and precious promises. These are the promises that enable you to share his divine nature and escape the world's corruption caused by human desires.

In view of all this, make every effort to respond to God's promises.

—2 PETER 1:4-5

TODAY'S THOUGHT

Doubt doesn't mean you have less faith but that your faith is being challenged in a new way. When you have moments of doubt, you are probably in unfamiliar territory. Allow doubt to move you closer to God, not farther away from him. God gives you many wonderful promises in the Bible, and he invites you to respond to those promises. Because he has fulfilled all of his promises, you can learn to trust instead of doubt. Then you will be even stronger in your faith.

TODAY'S PLAN

How can your faith grow through the process of dealing with doubt?

COMPASSION

TODAY'S PROMISE

Feed the hungry, and help those in trouble. Then your light will shine out from the darkness, and the darkness around you will be as bright as noon.

—ISAIAH 58:10

TODAY'S THOUGHT

God promises that those who help the poor will be rewarded, both in this life and the next. God has compassion for the poor and needy, so as a follower of God, you must also have compassion for them. Compassion that does not reach as far as your checkbook or your to-do list is not godly compassion. Godly compassion requires action. Helping those less fortunate than you is not merely an obligation but a privilege that should bring you great joy.

TODAY'S PLAN

What can you do this week to show compassion to someone who is poor or needy?

CHANGE

TODAY'S PROMISE

We have a priceless inheritance—an inheritance that is kept in heaven for you, pure and undefiled, beyond the reach of change and decay. —1 PETER 1:4

TODAY'S THOUGHT

One thing that never changes is that things change. You can't always control change, either for better or worse. But God and his Word never change, and his promises never change either! This gives you the assurance that every one of God's promises will come true, including the promise of eternal life in heaven. There you will never again see anything change for the worse.

TODAY'S PLAN

How can trusting in God's unchanging Word and promises for the future help you to cope with change today?

JUSTICE

TODAY'S PROMISE

Then at last everyone will say, "There truly is a reward for those who live for God; surely there is a God who judges justly here on earth." —PSALM 58:11

TODAY'S THOUGHT

When you are experiencing difficult times, it is tempting to think God is not fair or just. How can he allow a Christian to suffer when so many unbelievers are prospering? The Bible tells us that justice and fairness will often be perverted in this life by selfish people. But God promises that justice will not be twisted forever. True justice will one day prevail in eternity for those who live for God.

TODAY'S PLAN

Do you trust that God's justice will one day prevail?

DISTRACTIONS

TODAY'S PROMISE

Jesus told him, "Anyone who puts a hand to the plow and then looks back is not fit for the Kingdom of God."

—LUKE 9:62

TODAY'S THOUGHT

Distractions take your focus off Jesus. You might be doing great things, but if you take your eyes off Jesus, even for a moment, you could stumble. God's enemies work hard to distract you. They will try everything to get your mind off of God and onto sin. If temptation can turn your head even for a minute, it puts you in danger of swerving off the path of righteousness. Many other things can distract you from your walk with God—busyness, material things, problems, even good things. If you are aware of these distractions, you can try to minimize them so you stay on course in following God.

TODAY'S PLAN

How can you minimize the distractions that keep you from focusing on the road God wants you to take?

DECEMBER

GIVING

TODAY'S PROMISE

God has given each of you a gift from his great variety of spiritual gifts. Use them well to serve one another.
— 1 PETER 4:10

TODAY'S THOUGHT

Giving is sharing something you own—time, talents, finances—with someone else. In a deeper sense, giving is sharing something of yourself. Giving originates with the God who gives more blessings to his people than they deserve or expect. He gives the gift of life, the gift of love, the gift of salvation, the gift of eternity in heaven—all priceless gifts. God also gives us spiritual gifts that we should use to serve each other. The Bible promises that the more we give, the more we will receive—not necessarily in material possessions, but in spiritual and eternal rewards.

TODAY'S PLAN

How can you give of yourself to someone else today?

HOLINESS

TODAY'S PROMISE

Even before he made the world, God loved us and chose us in Christ to be holy and without fault in his eyes.
—EPHESIANS 1:4

TODAY'S THOUGHT

God does not regard you as holy because you are sinless but because Jesus died to take your sins away. Only Jesus Christ has lived a sinless life, but anyone who seeks forgiveness for sin and acknowledges Jesus as Savior and Lord becomes holy and sincerely tries to live in obedience to God's Word. Because of Jesus, God sees that person as holy. What an amazing thought! God sent his Son to die for your sins, and now he sees only holiness when he looks at you!

TODAY'S PLAN

Have you accepted God's forgiveness so that he now sees you as holy?

ETERNITY

God . . . has planted eternity in the human heart, but even so, people cannot see the whole scope of God's work from beginning to end.   —ECCLESIASTES 3:11

TODAY'S THOUGHT

God has "planted eternity in the human heart." This means that we instinctively know there is more than just this life. We feel that something is missing. Because we are created in God's image, we have eternal value, and nothing but the eternal God can truly satisfy. He has built into us a restless yearning for the kind of perfect world that can only be found in heaven. He gives us a glimpse of that world in some of the beautiful things we experience here on earth.

Someday he will restore earth to the perfection it had when he first created it. Eternity will be a never-ending exploration of its beauty in a perfect relationship with God.

TODAY'S PLAN

When you look around you today, do you see any glimpses of the perfect world that awaits you?

HEAVEN

TODAY'S PROMISE

Jesus told him, "I am the way, the truth, and the life. No one can come to the Father except through me."

—JOHN 14:6

TODAY'S THOUGHT

Jesus is the only way to heaven—that's a promise. You may want to buy your way in, work your way in, or think your way in. But the Bible is clear— Jesus Christ provides the only way in. Believing and gratefully accepting this truth is the only way to get to life's most important destination.

TODAY'S PLAN

Have you been counting on something other than Jesus to get you into heaven?

CHANGE

TODAY'S PROMISE

God is working in you, giving you the desire and the power to do what pleases him. —PHILIPPIANS 2:13

TODAY'S THOUGHT

God doesn't force change on you. When you invite him into your life, you give him permission to use his power to change you. If you try to change on your own, you won't get good results, but you will get discouraged. Instead, let the very power of God himself begin a work of transformation in you that will last a lifetime. Your life will see dramatic changes if you allow God to do his work in you.

TODAY'S PLAN

How can you allow God to change you from the inside out?

HOPE

TODAY'S PROMISE

She will have a son, and you are to name him Jesus, for he will save his people from their sins.

—MATTHEW 1:21

TODAY'S THOUGHT

Your greatest hope is that because of Jesus, you will live forever in heaven with God. Until that hope is fulfilled, God has a plan for you to carry out in your life here and now. Listen to God and follow him closely so that you can fulfill his plan for you, just as Jesus fulfilled God's plan for him.

TODAY'S PLAN

Ask God each day to reveal his plans for you, and never lose hope that he is working out his purposes in your life.

COMPASSION

TODAY'S PROMISE

He will rescue the poor when they cry to him; he will help the oppressed, who have no one to defend them. He feels pity for the weak and the needy . . . for their lives are precious to him. —PSALM 72:12-14

TODAY'S THOUGHT

A mark of godliness is reflecting God's compassionate heart to others. If you want to be like him, you must develop a heart of compassion and the discipline of helping those in need.

TODAY'S PLAN

How can you learn more about God's compassion so you can show more compassion to others?

NEEDS

TODAY'S PROMISE

Don't be like them, for your Father knows exactly what you need even before you ask him! —MATTHEW 6:8

TODAY'S THOUGHT

God promises to supply your needs, not your wants. You will never be content if you focus on your wants because you will always want more. The more you focus on what God values, the more you will be able to distinguish your wants from your needs. If you never feel content, you may be focusing too much on what you want instead of discovering what God knows that you need.

TODAY'S PLAN

How does knowing that God takes care of all your needs influence what you want?

LONELINESS

TODAY'S PROMISE

Nothing can ever separate us from God's love. No power in the sky above or in the earth below—indeed, nothing in all creation will ever be able to separate us from the love of God that is revealed in Christ Jesus our Lord.

—ROMANS 8:38-39

TODAY'S THOUGHT

In the dark hours of the night, do you feel desperately alone and rejected? Perhaps a best friend deserted you. The marriage you hoped for never materialized. Or the person you married now wants out. Maybe your child has turned against you, or your parents and friends don't seem to care. But God says, "Do not be afraid, for I am with you" (Isaiah 43:5). God promises to love you no matter what.

TODAY'S PLAN

Do you feel God's presence and his love even when you are all alone?

ABANDONMENT

TODAY'S PROMISE

*Those who know your name trust in you, for you,
O LORD, do not abandon those who search for you.*

—PSALM 9:10

TODAY'S THOUGHT

There may be times when even those closest to you
will neglect or even abandon you, but God never
will. He promises that he will never abandon you
when you look for him. When you are feeling
deserted and alone, it may be just the right time
to look more intently and see that God is there
by your side. God is always trying to get your
attention. Are you aware of him? If you are sincerely seeking him, you are sure to find him.

TODAY'S PLAN

*How have you felt God's presence even when others aban-
doned you?*

PATIENCE

TODAY'S PROMISE

God is pleased with you when you do what you know is right and patiently endure unfair treatment. Of course, you get no credit for being patient if you are beaten for doing wrong. But if you suffer for doing good and endure it patiently, God is pleased with you.
—1 PETER 2:19-20

TODAY'S THOUGHT

God uses your life's circumstances to develop your patience. You can't always choose your circumstances, but you can choose how you respond to them. God promises that he is pleased when you are patient in the midst of difficult circumstances. Patience is not a virtue when you are suffering the consequences of doing something wrong, but patience pleases God when you are suffering unfairly or for doing good.

TODAY'S PLAN

Have can you respond to your life's circumstances with more patience?

CHANGE

TODAY'S PROMISE

All of us who have had that veil removed can see and reflect the glory of the Lord. And the Lord—who is the Spirit—makes us more and more like him as we are changed into his glorious image.

—2 CORINTHIANS 3:18

TODAY'S THOUGHT

The more time that two people spend together, the more alike they become. They adopt certain figures of speech or accents of the other person. They sometimes begin to dress alike or even think alike. The same is true when you spend more and more time with Jesus. Soon your speech becomes gentle and kind, your face mirrors his joy, your attitudes and motives become more pure, and your actions become more focused on serving others. When Christ changes you, it's always for the better!

TODAY'S PLAN

Can other people see you becoming more and more like Jesus every day?

COMMUNICATION

TODAY'S PROMISE

You can be sure of this: The LORD set apart the godly for himself. The LORD will answer when I call to him.
—PSALM 4:3

Because of Christ and our faith in him, we can now come boldly and confidently into God's presence.
—EPHESIANS 3:12

TODAY'S THOUGHT

People like to keep in touch because it is vital to the quality and success of any relationship, whether marriage, friendship, family, or business. The same principle applies to your relationship with God. You must find ways to communicate with him, and you must learn to listen as he communicates with you. The more time you spend communicating with God, the closer and more successful your relationship with him will be.

TODAY'S PLAN

What can you do to keep in touch with God today?

PRESENCE OF GOD

Come close to God, and God will come close to you.

—JAMES 4:8

If someone gave you a free pass to an event, you wouldn't hesitate to go. You would have the privilege of admission because of the generosity of the giver. Your faith in Jesus Christ is God's free pass into his presence. When you put your trust in Jesus, you can enter God's presence with confidence. As you come close to him, he promises to draw close to you.

Have you accepted God's free pass to come into his presence and be close to him?

CONFUSION

TODAY'S PROMISE

Fix your thoughts on what is true, and honorable, and right, and pure, and lovely, and admirable. Think about things that are excellent and worthy of praise. Keep putting into practice all you learned. . . . Then the God of peace will be with you.

—PHILIPPIANS 4:8-9

TODAY'S THOUGHT

Life is less confusing when you realize and accept that God truly is in control. The purpose of God's control is not to manipulate you or order you around but to assure you that this world is not random and chaotic. If that were the case, life would be meaningless. But because God is in control of the world, you can be sure his promises will come true. You can live a life of purpose rather than confusion and make a difference for all eternity. Then you will be at peace.

TODAY'S PLAN

Do you really believe God is in control? How can this belief decrease your confusion and increase your peace of mind?

SERVICE

TODAY'S PROMISE

[Jesus said,] "Remain in me, and I will remain in you. For a branch cannot produce fruit if it is severed from the vine, and you cannot be fruitful unless you remain in me. Yes, I am the vine; you are the branches. Those who remain in me, and I in them, will produce much fruit. For apart from me you can do nothing." —JOHN 15:4-5

TODAY'S THOUGHT

When you are connected to Jesus, he turns your simple acts of service into something profound and purposeful. For example, he turns your simple act of singing into a profound chorus of praise that ministers to an entire congregation. He turns your simple act of telling others your testimony of faith into a profound moment in the heart of a friend who suddenly realizes his need for salvation. Stay connected to Jesus, and let him turn your simple acts of service into profound works for the Kingdom of God.

TODAY'S PLAN

What simple act of service can you do for Jesus today?

PEACE

TODAY'S PROMISE

You will keep in perfect peace all who trust in you, all whose thoughts are fixed on you! —ISAIAH 26:3

TODAY'S THOUGHT

There are many ways to achieve peace, or the semblance of peace, but genuine peace is found only in a trusting relationship with God. Peace is not the absence of conflict but the presence of God. Peace of mind comes as the Holy Spirit guides you into God's purposes for your life and gives you an eternal perspective. Peace of heart comes as the Holy Spirit guides you into a productive life and comforts you in times of trouble.

TODAY'S PLAN

Where are you looking for peace? Are you looking in the right place?

GIFTS

TODAY'S PROMISE

God loved the world so much that he gave his one and only Son, so that everyone who believes in him will not perish but have eternal life. —JOHN 3:16

TODAY'S THOUGHT

The greatest gift God gives you is his Son. Through his gift of Jesus, he also gives you the gift of eternal life. What makes these gifts so wonderful is that you don't have to work for them or earn them. You simply believe that God has actually given you his Son and the offer of eternal life with him. Then you accept the gifts. And no one can take them away.

TODAY'S PLAN

God has given you gifts too wonderful to keep to yourself. Whom can you share them with?

SHARING

TODAY'S PROMISE

When Christ, who is your life, is revealed to the whole world, you will share in all his glory. —COLOSSIANS 3:4

TODAY'S THOUGHT

Ever since we were little children, we've been taught to share. Yet for most of us, it remains as hard as ever to share either our things or ourselves. Why? Because at the very core of our sinful human nature is the desire to get, not give; to accumulate, not relinquish; to look out for ourselves, not for others. The Bible calls you to share many things—your resources, your faith, your love, your time, your talents, your money. It promises that those who share generously will discover the benefits of giving, which are far greater than the temporary satisfaction of receiving. God was willing to share his own Son with you so that you could have eternal life. When you realize how much God has shared with you, you will be more willing to share with others to bless their lives.

TODAY'S PLAN

What do you have that you can share generously with others?

WISDOM

For a child is born to us, a son is given to us. The government will rest on his shoulders. And he will be called: Wonderful Counselor, Mighty God, Everlasting Father, Prince of Peace. —ISAIAH 9:6

TODAY'S THOUGHT

If you are fortunate, you have someone you can always depend on for good advice. You are even more blessed when that person is not only wise and godly but loving and caring as well, and always willing to give you as much time as you need. Jesus can be that kind of counselor in your life. He came for the purpose of giving you loving, caring, perfect counsel that will carry you through life into eternity.

TODAY'S PLAN

Do you seek the counsel of Jesus when you need wisdom?

VICTORY

TODAY'S PROMISE

The Mighty One is holy, and he has done great things for me. He shows mercy from generation to generation to all who fear him. His mighty arm has done tremendous things! —LUKE 1:49-51

TODAY'S THOUGHT

It's hard to picture the baby Jesus as the mighty God, but he was mighty enough to create the world, live a sinless life, heal countless people, calm storms, and conquer death. He is mighty enough to conquer your troubles, too. Jesus promises to give you ultimate victory!

TODAY'S PLAN

Do you see Jesus only as a meek and lowly baby or as a mighty warrior and victorious Savior?

RISK

TODAY'S PROMISE

Mary responded, "I am the Lord's servant. May everything you have said about me come true." And then the angel left her. —LUKE 1:38

TODAY'S THOUGHT

Take the risk of doing things God's way. When God asks you to follow him, he won't necessarily give you all the information up front. When you step out in faith, he gives you just enough guidance to see where to take the next step. Mary risked her marriage, her reputation, and her future by becoming the mother of Jesus. Following God's will is not without risks, but God promises that it is the greatest reward.

TODAY'S PLAN

How much risk are you willing to take in following God?

ANGELS

He will order his angels to protect you wherever you go. They will hold you up with their hands so you won't even hurt your foot on a stone. —PSALM 91:11-12

TODAY'S THOUGHT

The Bible does not say whether there is one specific "guardian angel" assigned to each believer. It does say that God uses his angels to counsel, guide, protect, minister to, rescue, fight for, and care for his people. Whether he uses one specific angel or a whole host of angels to help you is his choice and your blessing. Chances are that angels have played a greater role in your life than you realize. Thank God today for the supernatural ways he cares for you.

TODAY'S PLAN

How will knowing that God sends his angels to be involved in your life affect the way you act today?

SALVATION

TODAY'S PROMISE

The Savior—yes, the Messiah, the Lord—has been born today in Bethlehem, the city of David! And you will recognize him by this sign: You will find a baby wrapped snugly in strips of cloth, lying in a manger.

—LUKE 2:11-12

TODAY'S THOUGHT

God often accomplishes his plans in unexpected ways. God used the census of a Roman emperor to bring Joseph and Mary to Bethlehem. He chose to have Jesus born in a stable rather than a palace; he chose tiny Bethlehem rather than the capital, Jerusalem; and he chose to proclaim the news of Jesus' birth first to shepherds rather than to kings. Perhaps God did all this to show that life's greatest treasure—salvation through Jesus—is available to everyone, no matter what their status.

TODAY'S PLAN

Have you accepted the salvation that Jesus brought to all people?

DECEMBER 25

TIMING OF GOD

TODAY'S PROMISE

When we were utterly helpless, Christ came at just the right time and died for us sinners. —ROMANS 5:6

TODAY'S THOUGHT

God's people had been longing for the Messiah
for centuries, yet God sent Jesus to earth at just
the right time. We may not fully understand why
this was perfect timing until we get to heaven
and see God's complete plan. But you can be
sure that God sent Jesus at the time when the
most people, both present and future, would be
reached with the Good News of salvation.

TODAY'S PLAN

*How do you see evidence of God's perfect timing in your
life?*

RIGHTEOUSNESS

The LORD . . . hears the prayers of the righteous. . . . The godly run to him and are safe. . . . The godly are as bold as lions. —PROVERBS 15:29; 18:10; 28:1

The righteous will shine like the sun in their Father's Kingdom. —MATTHEW 13:43

TODAY'S THOUGHT

Those who are righteous, or godly, in God's eyes are: safe in his care—their souls cannot be snatched away by Satan; bold in his work—they have the courage to do the right thing and are not ashamed of their faith; persistent in prayer—they enjoy close fellowship with God; and outwardly radiant from inner beauty—others can see they are different and are attracted to what they see in them. God promises all these things to you when you are righteous before him through faith in his Son, Jesus.

TODAY'S PLAN

Does God consider you to be righteous?

FUTURE

TODAY'S PROMISE

The LORD directs our steps, so why try to understand everything along the way?
—PROVERBS 20:24

TODAY'S THOUGHT

God reveals just enough of the future to increase your dependence on him. God alone knows everything about the future, and he wants you to be a part of his work in it, so you must rely on him to lead you there. That is the essence of what it means to live by faith. Faith is trusting God to lead you into the future he promises you rather than trying to create your own future by yourself.

TODAY'S PLAN

Are you charting your own future, or are you following God into the future he has for you?

EQUALITY

TODAY'S PROMISE

We are made right with God by placing our faith in Jesus Christ. And this is true for everyone who believes, no matter who we are. —ROMANS 3:22

TODAY'S THOUGHT

God's salvation is available to all people. It doesn't matter what sins you've committed. It doesn't matter who you are. God loves all people equally and wants everyone to be saved from eternal death and to live with him in heaven. When you decide to follow Jesus Christ and ask him to forgive your sins and make you a new person inside, he promises to look at you as though you have never sinned. In his eyes, you are clean and pure, just like everyone else who believes.

TODAY'S PLAN

How do God's love and offer of salvation make everyone equal? Have you been made right in God's eyes?

FAILURE

TODAY'S PROMISE

The LORD directs the steps of the godly. He delights in every detail of their lives. Though they stumble, they will never fall, for the LORD holds them by the hand. —PSALM 37:23-24

TODAY'S THOUGHT

Don't let failure get you down; see it instead as a good way to grow and mature. When you fail, you must get up and try again. Many inspiring success stories tell of people who failed many times but who never gave up. Most important, you must never give up on your relationship with God. He promises you the ultimate success of gaining salvation and eternal life.

TODAY'S PLAN

What failures have you experienced lately? How can you turn them into successes?

GENEROSITY

TODAY'S PROMISE

The same Lord . . . gives generously to all who call on him. —ROMANS 10:12

TODAY'S THOUGHT

God has generously offered you the gift of life forever in a perfect world, with the promise of riches beyond measure. All you have to do is accept and believe that he's really giving you such a magnificent gift. If God were not a generous and compassionate God, he might require his followers to work for their salvation, or he might give only a privileged few the chance to get into heaven. But God is generous, and he offers the same gift to everyone who comes to him.

TODAY'S PLAN

Have you accepted the generous gift God is offering you?

DECEMBER 31

SERVICE

TODAY'S PROMISE

Among you it will be different. Whoever wants to be a leader among you must be your servant, and whoever wants to be first among you must be the slave of everyone else.

—MARK 10:43-44

TODAY'S THOUGHT

A popular conception of wealth and success is being able to afford the luxury of having servants. Jesus turns this thinking on its head by teaching that the highest goal in life is to be a servant. He places such a high value on serving because it is centered on others rather than yourself, and serving others is the essence of effective Christian living. God promises that those who serve others will be the most highly regarded in his Kingdom.

TODAY'S PLAN

How can you serve God today by humbly serving someone else?

TOPICAL INDEX

Scripture Index

Do-able. Daily. Devotions.

IT'S EASY TO GROW WITH GOD THE ONE YEAR WAY.

The One Year Mini for Women helps women connect with God through several Scripture verses and a devotional thought. Perfect for use anytime and anywhere between regular devotion times. Hardcover.

The One Year Mini for Students offers students from high school through college a quick devotional connection with God anytime and anywhere. Stay grounded through the ups and downs of a busy student lifestyle. Hardcover.

The One Year Mini for Moms provides encouragement and affirmation for those moments during a mom's busy day when she needs to be reminded of the high value of her role. Hardcover.

The One Year Mini for Busy Women is for women who don't have time to get it all done but need to connect with God during the day. Hardcover.

The One Year Mini for Men helps men connect with God anytime, anywhere between their regular devotion times through Scripture quotations and a related devotional thought. Hardcover.

The One Year Mini for Leaders motivates and inspires leaders to maximize their God-given leadership potential using scriptural insights. Hardcover.